CW01021407

The Diary Of A Warless Warrior

02/06/10 - 08/11/10

A Book Of The Blog
www.1nomad.blogspot.com

by Mike Jones

The Diary And Path Of The Warless Warrior

The following is dedicated to my long suffering family and friend.
A recent addition to those I'd like to thank, have been my long johns. Thank you for your precious warmth, and thank you T.K Maxx for only charging me a tenner for them I understand now why a mans age was counted in the number of winters he'd survived... Thank you Reader, please do enjoy...

Wednesday 02/06/10

A famous Diarist by the name Pepys once wrote "a day unrecorded is a day wasted". I do agree to an extent, but I also think he was pretty biased towards his fact recording hobby. If it wasn't for Pliny the erm..Younger? Elder? one of them anyhow, the eruption of Pompeii would remain that much more mysterious.

I have resolved henceforth to record my days activities. For posterity, for wealth (I think not), for fun, we'll see.

I am a 24 year old, currently employed with a partner and child. There are a fair few of us out there, thankfully, not all like me.

So. This morning, I overslept. Despite only being ten minutes after the time I should've arrived, I took a day for the Queen, otherwise known as a duvet day... although there wasn't much duvet today. Took Emma, my partner, to work, then went about researching the recipe for nettle beer, and proceeded to pick 100 nettle tops. Why? Because I'm currently reading The Tree House Diaries by Nick Weston and have taken it upon myself to test the recipes he describes.

Nettle beer

- 100 nettle tops (with leaves 4-6)
- 12 litres (2 ½ gallons) water
- 1 ½ kg (3lb) sugar
- 50g cream of tartar
- 15g brewers or beer yeast

After my foraging I returned home to realise I was without Cream of Tartar. The whole 50g of it that was required. So off I went to town. The problem is I'm a great believer when it comes to burning my black gold aka fuel/oil in always getting more than one job done, so soon I had a long list. Chuck in some impulse buys like a wind up torch/charger, sixteen AAA batteries, a large stock pot, and by god you've just spent nigh on eighty pounds!

To make myself feel better for the expenses and todays loss of earnings, I've listed my 'as new' SAT Nav on eBay. Lets hope it does well!

My mate Luke popped up to kill time and help me scout a good camp site for this weekend. In the end we collected the women and made an evening of it by ordering pizza. The highlight also being my opportunistic shooting of a jackdaw perching on our aerial, sadly I only winged it. Before I could despatch it as quickly and humanely as possible, Bill, the next door neighbours cat nicked it and finished it off somewhere in the bushes. Bugger me did the rooks and other jackdaws go NUTS! Was like a scene from 'The Birds'.

Knackered now, best not lose any more of next months pay check!

Thursday 03/06/10

Actually made it into work today, and quickly wished I hadn't. Recently management had a cost cutting brainwave, take vehicles off the road, make the staff work longer and harder. All under the guise of cutting fuel usage and CO_2 emissions.

I work on recycling collection. You'd be forgiven for thinking we used electric-hybrid trucks, or at least bio-diesel. No. These clapped out trucks are nearly 10 years old and 'hand me downs' from other contracts. They do 8 miles to the gallon and still management are happy to send such a gas guzzler 10 miles or more to collect ONE box because one lazy bastard didn't put it out early enough and had the gall to complain to the council. Rather than say "tough titties" Veolia (the recycling contractor) will still send a massive kerbsider for it as a missed box incurs a £40 penalty, so they say...

We get paid for ten hours regardless of whether we finish after 6 or 8 hours and then go home. But they have understandably decided to get their moneys worth by increasing the size of the rounds to 1200 plus properties. So in sweltering conditions, we loaded 8 tonnes of crap bound for china for 10 hours 6am - 4:30pm.
Got home with a strained back muscle, a sunburnt neck and face as well as severe dehydration...
Had a bath then tea, now its bedtime. oh and had to pick Emma's dad up, bring him over, then run him back. I'm shagged out, and now raring to do it all again.

Just living the dream...

Friday 04/06/10

Just another day at the Office...

Got up as required, got carried away checking the bank balance and was late leaving by 15 minutes.

Was hardly worth rushing as we only got pissed around anyway. I hate work. Its not because I'm work shy, I assure you. Employment is ridiculous and unnatural.

Think about it. Instead of spending the day doing things essential to our living and survival, we spend at least 8 hours a day, 5 days a week doing the same task over and over. So rather than doing many varied tasks and activities, we sell our souls and time for gold to pay someone else for something you could have made/done yourself and perpetuate the cycle.

Is it any wonder depression is so common? Unfortunately if everyone had my desire to not earn and rather, work to live, the Government would have a severe income problem!

Wanted to sod off and go camping, but had loads of cleaning and washing up to do. Didn't finish the chores til gone 7pm. Settled for making a fire in the garden, and falling asleep by it. Got pretty cold so jacked it in.

Off to Wales tomorrow to visit the Lammas Project. An Eco village/ Smallholding jobby. Should be interesting, might get to go camping in time for the weather to turn shit....

Will let ya know.

Saturday 05/06/10 - Wednesday 09/06/10

WOW!

What an adventure! Went to Lammas as planned, had a great day. Left, car broke down! Retreated to a petrol station we'd passed (car would start, appear to be fine, then die) and filled up in case of dodgy fuel, then tried again. Same thing at exactly the same place which happened to be the sign reading "Welcome to Carmarthenshire". Check engine light would flash then engine would lose power and die. Decided to return to Lammas as a point of reference for the RAC, plus we wouldn't be on our own.

Ended up staying with a fantastic family for the best part of three days and have now decided to live there with them!

I cannot describe the feeling we've been left with. A calling. My soul has awakened. My energy is channelled. At Lammas we'll be growing our food and building a house...first steps are to fix car, sell/swap for camper/caravan. Sell our crap. Easy!

Just have to slug out our jobs for another month or two.

Now I have the system by the balls and not the other way around.

Paul W running us through his build and explaining the planning battle

The Mill Pond

The Diary And Path Of The Warless Warrior

Nigel and Cassies reciprocal roof.

View across the valley from Simon D's plot

The Diary And Path Of The Warless Warrior

Morning at Lammas, Tir-Y-Gafel

Mill pond in the morning at Lammas, Tir-Y-Gafel

The Diary And Path Of The Warless Warrior

A peek inside Simon D and Jasmine's House

The Slug Refuge...

Thursday 10/06/10

Went to work. Bloody tough day. Also finding it really hard to keep focussed. I JUST WANT TO QUIT AND GET ON WITH THINGS!!!!!

Spoke to my parents who seem really quite supportive, which I definitely did not expect. They advised us to buy a caravan rather than a camper van. Bid on one on eBay that evening for £200 with awning. Will probably lose it to someone with deeper pockets.

Emma's Mum is now on board and she says her Nan is willing to help financially. I have a fair few concerns. Lots of thoughts flying around right now, doubt I'll sleep well.

NOT looking forward to being pissed about at work tomorrow. Hate my job now. Stops me doing what I need to do to get on with my life.

11

Home - For the foreseeable future...

Tuesday 15/06/10

Boy am I pooped! Been a hectic few days. Am doing my best not to let days go past unrecorded but it seems I need to be a bit more disciplined.

Handed my notice in Friday, with no intention of serving the one week required. I did warn the boss I would contract a "mysterious and intense" 4 day long illness that might dent my attendance record. The message obviously wasn't communicated judging by the phone call today from my rather annoyed supervisor. I did consider going in but soon thought better of it when I realised my core motive for doing so would be money. NO. I refuse to sell out to the system.

When I handed my notice in I'd calculated that the days I'd worked plus the holiday accrued was enough to fund my direct debits which I shall soon be cancelling.

To have gone in and suffered because of greed for gold would have been negating the point of this entire exercise.

That said, I am prepared that should the shit hit the fan and the money raised from the sale of our belongings not be enough, I would work a short period. But that scenario is exceedingly unlikely if we stick to the plan...

Saturday was supposed to be spent preparing for the car boot sale Sunday. Instead we bought a caravan I'd seen with a FOR SALE sign and £200 pegged to a curtain. The owner randomly, and very kindly lowered the price to £150 and we were in for one hell of a bargain!

4 berth, good condition, WITH awning and poles!

Turns out it was her late fathers, but get this, when I mentioned to her brother I was after a 4x4 he gestured over his shoulder to a rough and ready looking Land Rover Discovery! He initially said he wanted £800/£750 for it but admitted it needed a new water pump. I text later on the Monday and lied I'd only been offered £500 for my car so could he meet me at £600, he agreed!

Got £600 for my Galant on eBay and better still, found a water pump for a Discovery for £15! The gods appear to be on my side (at present)

Now whilst the sale of my car has gone pretty smoothly so far (being paid for and picked up Friday I hope) Emma's car has been a different story... hopefully it'll sell for £250 a snip considering we paid £750 barely a year ago for it!

The car boot sale went okay I suppose. Overslept which didn't help but got rid of perhaps half the stuff we took and made £32 profit, promptly swallowed at the petrol pump along with £19 more of my meaningless currency. Took all the unsold stuff to the charity shop....

Anyhoo. Solar panels arrived today from Maplin god bless em. £199.99 60watts. Just need a proper battery for it Also need to work out how the electrics go together in the caravan. I have a hunch I know where the switch is...

Wednesday 16/06/10

Bit of a rough day. Only due to a tiff with Emma. Started out ok, dropped Frances, my daughter, at school, Emma at work.

Came back, had a shave with my new cut throat razor. Only the 2nd time I've used it and not a nick yet! Then a soak in the tub. By the time I'd cleaned out my ears it was getting on for 10/10:30. Hopped out, packaged up some PC games I'd sold then off to the Post Office and over to my parents to return their laptop from being fixed by Emma's colleague. Also took over a digital photo frame about 6 months after I bought it for them. God I'm crap sometimes.

Had a bite and a chat then off to pick Emma up so she could grab some lunch at home.

I was then overwhelmed with siesta syndrome and succumbed by napping on the sofa whilst Em had a sarnie. Must've given the impression that's all I currently do all day!

Tiff started over glass and plastic. I know. Out of context its ridiculous, even in context its stupid. Emma said we could keep our water in glass demi johns whereas my idea was to use one of my plastic brewing barrels with a tap and is 5 times the size. My argument was based on weight, hers on something her mother had said about plastic leeching chemicals. I was also talking broadly due to the legal restrictions on towing and 'train weight'.

Anyhoo. Without a word of thanks from Emma for our midday rendezvous and taxiing, I decided she could walk home. Weather was fantastic plus it'd free me up to actually get something useful done.

After picking up Frances from school I finally got round to sorting through and emptying my wardrobe. 4 bin bags worth! Might try and sell at a car boot sale this weekend but they're most likely headed for the charity shop.

Luke came up for a chat and to chill. Always a pleasure.
Can't wait to do something else tomorrow that can summon my dream forward into reality. Even if it is just by one small step.

Thursday 17/06/10

Not much to report today really. Did the usual taxiing then came home and watched 'Slumming it' with Kevin McCloud. Interesting stuff.

Intended to clean the car inside and out at my parents. Decided to do it tomorrow as Uncle Ken arrived two minutes after we did (Fran & I).

Watched France vs Mexico world cup game - Wanted Mexico to win. Have always liked them after watching I think the '94 world cup when Campos played for them. He was so entertaining. A striker who could also go in goal. He was a brilliant little guy... Anyhoo they won 2:0 (Mexico)

Friday (At Last) 18/06/10

A sale. A purchase.

After attending my daughters "work of the week" assembly. I took the opportunity to call on our friends Andy and Bridget, with an ulterior motive... Aside from a hot brew, I desired the use of a pressure washer and a hoover. They kindly obliged and I cleaned my Mitsubishi Galant inside and out in preparation for the eBayer who would be purchasing it.

Really nice chap came, seemed pretty genuine, paid the agreed £600 in cash & left.

I then took that cash and bought the Land Rover Discovery an hour later. Need to get the water pump replaced but will attempt that myself if the part arrives in the post. Should save me £50-£100!

All in all a pretty good day.

Lets see what tomorrow brings.

Saturday 19/06/10

Landy water pump came. Of course I was in the bath, and yes on my own as Emma and Fran had nipped out to the shops. Bloody typical.

15

My Dad came over with some anti freeze and coolant and to look at the engine and advised me not to bother doing it myself...

Kinda followed his advice. I took it to a mate. Unfortunately, and as I suspected. It wasn't the water pump. We drained, flushed, and refilled the coolant system, but still something was wrong. The landy didn't overheat, but the coolant was overflowing and becoming pressurized over the prescribed 15 psi.

A neighbour quickly diagnosed the problem. I've been sold a land rover with a blown head gasket. Bummer.

Anyhoo. Being as I got it so cheap (and its now clear why) I can afford to get it repaired. Gunna do some serious bargaining come Monday. My dad is picking us up tomorrow for a roast dinner. Yum Yum.

Tuesday 22/06/10

Disco Stu, for that is his name, is very poorly. So poorly in fact, I've replaced him. Instead, with the kind help of the mother in law, we have a Vauxhall Monterey aka Isuzu Trooper.

Disco Stu had a Pre-MOT which he passed, however, he has indeed blown a head gasket. The cylinder head has been sent off to be inspected for cracks. Poor Stu.

The Monterey had a most interesting owner. An 80 year old gentleman, who certainly knew his stuff, and whose business was selling law books on eBay. His wife loved our daughter and whilst the women chatted, I was led to the bottom of his house to a porta cabin wherein was stored an extraordinary record of British legal heritage. Handwritten and bound in leather, were many many volumes recounting writs of the king as far back as 1475! He had in fact purchased the collection from Earl Spencer, Princess Diana's brother, keen to flog the families treasures, apparently to "Live it up with some crumpet in Wales..." . Interesting.

Wednesday 23/06/10

Right I'm tired. Not done much though. My dad picked up Emma and Fran in the morning which left me free, and bored, having to stay housebound to wait for some estate agent to inspect the house. The very same agent who didn't bother to turn up. So now I have another day of lonely idleness to look forward to.

Disco Stu's cylinder head was warped! Had obviously been allowed to overheat in the past to such an extent that not only did the temperature deform solid metal but also melted a sensor and knackered the heat plugs. Still, I've been assured the whole lot will amount to no more than £400 so have relisted him on eBay at £1294. I hope I can make another £300 as I did on the Galant but if someone offers a grand I'll cut my losses and take it.

Watched England scrape a 1-0 victory against Slovenia. Bad news as it means we face ze Germans this Sunday. We're buggered in my opinion.

Watched a program called 'Erasing David' all about the information collected on us by corporations and the government. Scary shit man. He was a pillock though. He went 'on the run' from two private eyes he'd hired to track him down. His aim was to last 30 days... he lasted 18 after his wife called him and made him attend a baby scan which the P.I's knew about through some sneaky tactics. Typical. Brought down by a moody woman. So many great men have fallen that way. If the Creationists are to be believed the first was Adam... Samson's up there too, along with Greek and Roman heroes. Poor Bastards.

Thursday 24/06/10

Feels as though the dream is fading. Getting bogged down by the grinding routine of this 'modern' living. Alot of my thinking time today has been devoted to how I can also disappear from the radar. To the extent of wearing sunglasses and a balaclava in and around towns and cities. Bit of a paradox considering that by hiding your identity you then become more visible. Granted, no one knows who you are, but conversely, I doubt it would take long before Big Brother would want to find out... Muslim women get away with it, hmmm there's an idea...naaahh....

Our man in Wales called to cancel this weekends visit. Pretty huge blow as I was relying on it to regain focus and perspective. A reminder of what is waiting at the other end... Just have to try and find a way to use the weekend to do something constructive. Something to bring the dream that one step closer. The trouble is, with the way my tired mind and body is, all I want to do is wallow in this misery.

Nice weather today though....

Sunday 27/06/10

Friday was busy-ish, got the tracking and wheel alignment done on the new 4x4. Just as well too as we decided that we would go ahead and venture off to Wales in search of Tipi Valley.

We packed the necessary equipment in case we didn't find it as it is notoriously off the beaten track.

We got most of the way there before my phone battery died and I just drove on, navigating with a combination of instinct and Google maps memory.

We found a spot that felt bloody close to Tipi Valley and at around 22:00 pitched a tent and bedded down.

I awoke around 5am Saturday morning and had a scout around. All the signs were there. A row of vans and converted campers, cars with maps chargers etc, evidence of traditional crafts and woodworking.

Found some wood and got a fire going, for breakfast we had rice...quite a good porridge equivalent!

Filled our water bottles at an eerily deserted farmhouse save for the cat who had met us the previous night and guided us to our camping spot. Transpired the occupants were at Glastonbury!

By following the track we then knocked on the last farmhouse on the track where the owner informed us we were in the right place, here was the fabled Tipi valley!

Back to the car to gather our stuff and off to the 'Big Lodge'.

The Diary And Path Of The Warless Warrior

We were greeted by Henry, a young chap with dreadlocks who put on a brew and answered our endless stream of questions and listened to our story. He introduced us to Lola and her three children. She in turn invited us to join the whole (or rather the remainder) of the community who were off to the village fair. On the walk down we picked a 12 foot bramble for the competition of who could find the longest bramble...

I joined the Valley men in a football tournament and seriously paid the price. Ouch! Cramp set in quickly due to the heat.

After Carol the Drunk was evicted we had the Big Lodge to ourselves for the duration of our stay.

Another 5am start for me on the Sunday. For me, in this lifestyle, it seems right to start the day when the sunrises, and turn in when it sets.

Frances got to ride two of the three horses with Jaz, I'll probably be heading down to the Yurt of my team mate and fellow brewing enthusiast, Dan, to sample some of his much lauded Elderflower wine.

Another hot day so should be most refreshing, undecided as to whether we'll go back home this evening...

Wednesday 30/06/10

Stayed Monday and headed home

Stopped off at the services for a burger and coffee, a good slap of what we want to leave!

Forced back into the services a couple of junctions later, as the food left me battling my eyelids. Not only did I have a snooze, but so did Em and Fran. Sadly all we've done that's positive is head over to the caravan on Tuesday to stock it with dried stuff. Em & Fran were off work and school until the doctor could rule out this e-coli. Emma's Mum managed to pick it up on holiday with Fran . Means our forced march to Farnborough could be cancelled due to Emma's sister Nicola being paranoid of infection.

Hope her paranoia lasts as I can't be arsed.

Otherwise it's back to the drudgery of mainstream life...BORING. Am tired but I think not from exercise but just wanting the day to end. Would probably feel better if I were sleeping in the garden. Going to read my Primitive Living book as bedtime research.

Wednesday 21/07/10

Am pretty annoyed with myself for not being more disciplined and writing more often. My excuse should be I've been really busy, but this just isn't true. The busyness has been more sporadic.

There was the whole moving and ruthless shedding of worthless junk, including some important stuff, like my land rovers v5 registration document

Have now sold that damn discovery for £800, so lost £200. Buyer insisted on having it MOT'd. Cheeky bastard did his best to get me to pay for it too!

Today was Frances' last at her current school, which now frees her up, finally.

Thursday 22/07/10

Had a pretty relaxed day, bar the afternoon.

Morning was spent in blissful distraction finding little unimportant things to do in order to avoid the washing up.

Took Emma along with Fran to her friend Jaynes in South Cerney. Watched ALOT of TV...Packing it in while I still can!

On the way back I dropped off Em & Fran in town, and had to nip back and collect the money for the Land Rover. After handing pretty much all of it over to Emma for my share of the Monterey, I paid the rest into my heavily overdrawn account.

Luckily we ate cheaply that night having been invited for a meal down at my parents neighbours.

Whilst down there Fran, and subsequently Anne, Em and David ended up playing all sorts of instruments ranging from the recorder, piccolo, clarinet, tenor and some rather wonderful stringed instrument whose name escapes me.
Looked rather like a foot.....

All in all a good day.

Friday 23/07/10

Made the decision to try and spend the day in a constructive fashion. So it started with the washing up and ended with a trip to Attwoolls...

Bought £160 of mostly useful and essential stuff I.e. new 110ah leisure battery, wellies, compass, rain suit for Fran. Plus some eccentric things like an Aussie leather bush hat - sexy!

The latter part of the day was filled with a visit from my buddy Luke and piss arsing about with my air rifle which lead to discovering the culprit behind its recent inaccuracy - a wobbly barrel. Unfortunately being a cheapy £50 job a fair few years ago, the offending part was sealed and unable to be adjusted. Guess what I'm doing tomorrow...

The Diary And Path Of The Warless Warrior

My new Edgar brothers MOD 60 .177 Air rifle vs my old Beeman

Saturday 24/07/10

Got my new rifle! Wow is it a beast. Spent the day zeroing and letting it all settle in. Parked in Asda car park in Gloucester, so whilst I went to pick it up, Em & Fran went for a mooch and resupply. Joined them inside and went for a coffee and a cake.

We've been cramming in the modern conveniences recently such as McDonalds, KFC, and loads of TV and computer! 20:30 went out with the air rifle to see if I couldn't bag a pigeon in the church yard over the road. Turns out I couldn't. Wasn't disappointed though. I love wandering the fields as quietly as possible. In hunter mode, your eyes are everywhere, so for once, you notice all that's around you. You hear the different bird calls, notice the bats darting over your head. Am very eager to do more of that and am very excited to think of all the countryside that will be at my disposal in this new life of ours.

Sunday 25/07/10

After a lazy morning, went to Emma's mums for Sunday lunch. Stuffed myself and promptly curled up on the sofa for a snooze. Didn't last long...ended up watching Oliver Twist with Fran. Feeling pretty crap after catching one of those deadly strains of cold. The type that would fell all but the hardiest of individuals. Lucky I'm such a hero!

I maintain its Emma's fault. I'm a hot sleeper that wears the minimum in bed and normally starts the night with the bedding half on and half off. Now SHE insists I sleep to her right and because of the end of the bed she's chosen, this means I must sleep by the window. 1) This is most incredibly inconvenient. It means I have to clamber over her in the morning as I am normally the first up and 2) it means the cold air from the window is funnelled onto me through out the night. Due to my state of undress, this has resulted in a fatal cold.

Things are gunna change around here...!

Monday 26/07/10

Still suffering...At deaths door I think... Still like the hero I am I soldier on. Albeit with a little three hour nap at midday.

Another run to town and a quick trip to our friends to say goodbye. Last night Fran and I stayed up late watching the Simpsons online. Em was out drinking, the dirty stop out. To take the mick, she came home around 22:30, drummed me out of Frans bed and then watched me make and assemble ours. (Have to pack away each morning to enable us to have a sit down area. A big downside to living in a caravan!)

Moving day tomorrow! yey!

Tuesday 27/07/10

Alarm was set for 04:30. Optimistic I Know. Eventually stirred at 05:00. As predicted we overran my departure time of 06:00, instead leaving at 07:30. Inevitable when there are females in tow... and she still forgot the porridge

The journey down was slow but passed quickly. Punctuated by only one stop at the services for breakfast and a well deserved coffee. I hammered on and on to Emma about weight in the caravan when we moved in and the tyres told me how much she'd listened when I hitched the van up...women...

Arrived around 11:45 and pretty much hit the ground running. First off was the positioning of the van. Then I got it stable. But stable just is not good enough. IT MUST BE LEVEL!... on a f***ing wonky diagonal hill. Cheers.

Much strained jacking eventually led onto erecting the awning where I amused myself with innuendos aplenty. Poles, rods, shafts, holes, positions, tightness etc etc

Next was the solar array. Built the frame and wrestled with fitting the panels. Bloody charge controller was shot. So much so the battery cable overheated and became squidgy, the fuse melted and the crocodile clip started smoking...

I'm knackered...

Wednesday 28/07/10

Drove an hour to the nearest Maplin shop to replace the duff controller. Also took the opportunity to do a top up shop at the supermarket. Already pretty settled. Busied myself 'mulching' the willow beds. Basically this involves putting down recycled cardboard to keep the grass down then shovelling cow poo onto it. Good fun, with some music going...

Ayres, the guy we're helping, spent the day creating pathways and building bridges over drainage ditches.

Over the coming days alot of time will be spent preparing the site of the first build ensuring all materials are on hand.

The Diary And Path Of The Warless Warrior

Finally got round to shoring up our caravan door. The wood had come away from the hinge. A couple of nails, hammer, bit of flashing, tin snips and wayhey! Well, for the time being. May very well need to replace a large portion of the door with fresh wood, but time will tell.

Am eager to try out the solar shower, however... no sun... guess a boring old wash will have to do.

Tomorrow I have decided to construct a washing up table out of some pallets, and maybe a bench.

Anything we can do in the awning rather than in the caravan, will help keep people from having to dance around each other.

Thursday 29/07/10

Our Stainless Steel Pump Pot

Used the rocket stove instead of the gas this morning to boil the kettle. Took ages. Mostly down to the dew. Stove needs some tweaking anyway, still, did the job. Chucked the boiled water into a flask - instant caffeine shots. Right! Table time!

My Triumph.

Table was a resounding success. Quite chuffed with my recycling and engineering. Used one pallet, actually less because I was left with some nice kindling.

Next item and project. Shower. Used three lengths of hazel lashed together. Tested it out as well, passed, but needs tweaking. Height. Solar Shower needs to be raised. Covering. Tarp is ok but will probably need another.

Plus positioning is a factor. Am not concerned so much about nudity, but others exposure it...

Friday 30/07/10

Replaced a leg of the shower as one was too long and bent meaning it was nigh on impossible to wrap a tarp around. Hit upon a small idea. Remove the hose of the solar shower. Its about half a metre long and if you bend it, it forms a kink and stops the flow. It also means that to have the nozzle above your head, is to no longer be able to reach the tap...

Sunday 01/08/10

A glorious day for a wedding! Was amazing to see everyone dressed up and not in wellies!

A fantastic service under the oak tree by the mill pond followed by a buffet meal in the marquee. With food out of the way the traditional dancing got under way which I thoroughly enjoyed. Eventually the drumming began and I drank myself to sleep, Fantastic.

Monday 02/08/10

Laundry Day.. Took a trip to the 'local' town 20 odd miles away. Seemed hardly worth it for just one bag of dirty washing, but the café bought coffee helped.

Tuesday 03/08/10

Made a bench today. Similar to the washing up table in its design and construction.

Started the build!

Began by making a 'bunyip' essentially just a tube filled with water secured to two posts. This instrument acts as a spirit level between two points. Ayres cut out squares for the post footings whilst I dug part of the drainage trench.

The building site

Have two more volunteers starting work tomorrow, so looking forward to meeting and greeting.

Have set my alarm to start work nice and early. Am eager to keep the momentum going.

Wednesday 04/08/10

Todays building involved various aspects. Drainage, footings and the poles. Our two American volunteers, Dan and Bree, worked really hard and were most impressive. I finished off the extension of the perimeter drainage ditch and then worked with Bree and Emma digging the footings. Dan broke up the soil with the digging bar, Bree and myself scooped it out onto a sieve where Emma sorted out the rocks from the top soil.

Around 12:00 Em & I went off to Crymych for some lunch supplies, which we ate in the poly tunnel. When the sun comes out that thing gets unbearably hot!

After lunch work resumed. Emma stripped the bark off one of the supports, I tamped slate into the footing for foundation, whilst Dan and Bree worked some more on the drainage ditch. Ayres busied himself with various tasks but wasn't at 100% on account of suffering from man flu.

The Diary And Path Of The Warless Warrior

The Diary And Path Of The Warless Warrior

Thursday 05/08/10

Continued yesterdays building tasks in good weather. More tamping of foundations, digging the drainage trenches and pole stripping. Ayres was back to full strength after an early night. Hopefully will be laying the perforated pipe and covering with gravel to form the french drain, but am not sure as we're forecast rain until Sunday...

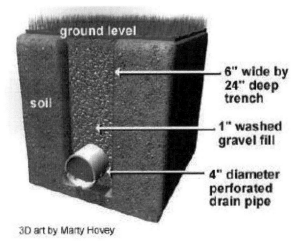

ground level

soil

6" wide by 24" deep trench

1" washed gravel fill

4" diameter perforated drain pipe

3D art by Marty Hovey

http://www.askthebuilder.com

Friday 06/08/10

Today was spent idling somewhat as rain stopped play. Decided to use the down time constructively and set about digitising my diary through a blog. On site is an agricultural building known as 'the clamp'. Here, residents pay for square footage for storage, but also a broadband connection. The electricity hook up is also used to charge depleted leisure batteries. In here I sat and typed until I felt hungry about 12:30/13:00 . After a quick refuel I then resumed my typing until 17:00 by which time my eyes were squiffy and I'd had enough.

At 20:30 I'd been told there would be a jamming session in the farmhouse so with an armful of firewood I set off. Things didn't really get going until 21:00 and by 22:00 I was ready to hit the hay. I find the rhythms that the group settle into put me into a deeply meditative state.

On my way back I saw Ayres was up and ended up smoking and chatting for an hour on the step outside the caravan. Witnessed a pretty damn impressive shooting star, if that's what it was, but you had to be there...

Saturday 07/08/10

This morning was a late one rising just after 09:00. Plan for the day ; Rubbish, gas, solar panels. Had a bit of a tiff with Emma as I felt her helping the build, then requiring me to help her around the home was diluting our roles and priorities. I am also mindful that if a helpful task such as washing up is done too regularly, it becomes the norm and expected.
I want to remain entirely focussed on what I am here to do.

Loaded up the wagon with empty gas canisters with Ayres, who incidentally was also in the middle of a tiff with his wife...women! Then got the rubbish and recycling on board. Issued with shopping lists, we were ready, just needed next door neighbour, Jude. This meant re jigging the back seat which resulted in a box of dead and decaying slugs falling out of a bag, then sliding down my arm. I brushed off the slime, disposed of the culprits, then joined Ayres at Judes. It was then it hit me. A waft of my arm. The vile stench of dead slug slime... Needless to say a quick scrub up was required. A thorough one too.

Dropped Ayres and Jude off at a farmers/agricultural shop then did my shopping. You can't rush in Wales. Not when there's a wedding on and the cashier is scurrying out of the shop between customers to try and catch a glimpse of the bride exiting the church.

Next stop, Nick the Gas. An Englishman who claimed to be nearly self sufficient bar items such as tea, sugar etc. Amazing bloke, off the cuff I asked if he could knock us up a gas bottle wood burner. His reply "tenner, will have it done by the end of the week". Cheers. We'll see a) if it does get done b) if it costs a tenner. To be fair I'm happy to pay way more than that.

Had a wander with the rifle at sunset. Nothing worth shooting. Did succeed in scaring the crap out of the neighbours who I called on to let them know their rear car window was wide open. In all honesty, to have a camo'd up stranger with a mahoosive rifle rock up to your caravan after sundown in Wales could be unnerving I suppose.

Sunday 08/08/10

Took the rifle and headed out a beautiful, clear and sunny morning. First off, I came across a small rucksack, upon inspection I found a child's change of clothes, a sleeping bag, and a y shaped stick. I think I know what the owner has in mind...

The Diary And Path Of The Warless Warrior

Next discovery was that of a camouflaged caravan nestled almost impossibly amongst the trees.

Was a useful exploration of the surrounding countryside.

The Diary And Path Of The Warless Warrior

The Diary And Path Of The Warless Warrior

Being a Sunday, the day has been pretty slow paced. I wandered over to the building site to break up some of the larger stones in the foundation footings. Not 5 minutes in, I managed to drop the whole weight of the tree stump I was using on my (formerly) big toe. Still haven't finished 'walking it off'.....

Helped out Kit whose wedding we attended with the clean up of the Marquee from 17:00-19:00, but aside from that chilled out.

A rare luxury was our pork joint for dinner, as meat has slipped down the menu and courgettes have taken over.

Monday 09/08/10

A very leisurely start to the day. Up around 09:00, finished breakfast and admin around 11:00. Still quite a novelty. although this will inevitably change when Frances returns to school and we effectively end up back in a weekday 9-5 routine. More tamping and foundation work. The slow start has been tolerated due to the weather. Started out grey and drizzly but at times unleashed some glorious sunshine. Rain returned at 17:15 which was convenient. Perhaps not if I end up going with the guys to play football.

Tuesday 10/08/10

Put in a good solid days work and completed digging out the drainage trench. The layout has now evolved so that the two channels join to a pond. This will not only serve to be an aesthetic garden feature, most likely housing fish, but will also reflect sunlight up into the house in accordance with permaculture principles.

Damn good thinking I say.

The evolution of the pond feature iterates the advantage of not building with architectural drawings and blueprints. The build is allowed to flow with ideas, which can manifest as and when circumstance allows. The end result is invariably unique and all the more beautiful.

The Diary And Path Of The Warless Warrior

These visitors just can't hack the pace.

Evening was spent around a washing machine drum fire and very quickly bedtime pounced.

Wednesday 11/08/10

Foundation pad with toe crushing tamper

Pipe in trench alongside polypropylene sack that will be used to create a silt barrier.

More tamping of foundation pads and now the perforated pipe has been laid. This is the basis of what is known as a French Drain, Essentially just a rubble trench, as with anything, there are many ways of achieving the same effect. The simplest is a gravel trench the most elaborate being with a pipe sock and eco textile lining.

Thursday 12/08/10

A day off, of sorts. Meeting my parents up in Llandovery to hand over Frances who'll be going on holiday with them to Devon until Sunday next.

Whilst there, will need to run a few errands and visit the laundrette. Evening was spent chatting to Ayres and his in laws. Another Meteor shower meant to be going on...

Friday 13/08/10

When you immerse yourself in a world of green building, it won't be long before you hear mention of reciprocal roofs. Well without experience of building these, I don't know much about them, but by God if I haven't just married that with my favourite commodity.. BEER!

Behold! The worlds first reciprocal fridge!

Saturday 14/08/10

A very pensive Ayres...

Birthday party! Celebrated Ayres' son Ellians birthday with a visit to the beach at Poppit sands. Weather was brilliant if a bit windy. Topped the day off with a rare luxury - Ice Cream! A Magnum Classic. Classic.

Sunday 15/08/10

Absolutely glorious weather. The sort of weather that beckons you to venture out. Emma and I took the opportunity to call upon some other plot holders. First stop was Paul and Hoppi's where Paul was engrossed in the creation of a family board game. This entailed a papier mache mountain range along with streams, meadows and 'forests' of gathered grasses. Was bloody impressed! Would appear to be Pauls calling to create awesome places people enjoy being involved in.

Had a few cups of tea and a good chat with Hoppi (Paul was in his element and far too involved lol) then it was off to talk beer with Kit and Saara.
Kit was extremely taken with my idea of a brewing co-operative and 'Man tent'. So we paid a visit to Simon D's whilst Emma and Saara gathered Rowan Berries.
Simon is no stranger to brewing and is in possession of a recipe book of all

sorts of weird and wonderful brews Sacred and Herbal Healing Beers: The Secrets of Ancient Fermentation.

His suggestion was to try using yarrow instead of hops or perhaps meadowsweet. He also allowed me to take one of his brewing kits, a Caxtons Best Bitter and some sugar and go off and start brewing! Yey! The Tir-Y-Gafel Brewers Co-operative has begun*. I'm interested to see how the brew pans out without the aid of my trusted 'Brew Belt'.

Kit invited us over for dinner, a potato curry. Most delicious. Have decided to go to Cardigan with Kit tomorrow to visit the brew shop.

Monday 16/08/10

Set off just after midday with Kit & Saara for a trip to Cardigan. Had a small shopping list from Ayres, but the main aim was to visit the brew shop. Of course it was shut on Mondays... So we filled the afternoon mooching around various shops, mostly charity ones collecting some pretty good bargains. I was particularly pleased with my purchase of two books: Brewing Beers Like Those You Buy and Amateur Winemaker recipes

The trip ended with a supermarket shop and then it was off to grab fish and chips in Crymych before us lads went off to play football in Maenclochog.

Had a good run around that saw us troop down to a seemingly near bankrupt village pub, and after another beer at Kits it was time to welcome the warm embrace of my bed and sweet restful slumber.

Tuesday 17/08/10

Had the morning to ourselves which was spent doing odd jobs and reading. Put in a couple of hours work on the gravel and the drainage trench from 14:00 - 17:30. After a bite of supper we headed over to a field by the community hub (Yurt) where a few of us played 'Ultimate Frisbee' led by the American visitors Dan and Bree. Was absolutely shattered by the time I hit the hay at 22:00.

Slugs share my 'spidey' sense for a good brew!

Wednesday 18/08/10

Another trip to Cardigan, again with Kit & Saara. This time with the wheel of Ayres' daughters bike, a bag of laundry and a visit to the brew shop. Despite having intentions of exploring a mash tun/boiler in order to make my beers from scratch. I have been dissuaded on two accounts by the shop owner. One, the price of hops £5.11 for 500g due to last years floods wiping out the crops in Kent. Two, the price of Barley and malt, now inflated as a result of the Russian crop failure, this time due to drought and water shortages.

After lots more mooching a trip to Tesco's and the reduced section yielded venison steaks!

An evening meal at Kit & Saara's wrapped things up nicely.

Thursday 19/08/10

My Dads birthday today, left a message... Put in some work on the building site which is now simply a case of filling a barrow of sifted stone and dumping it in a trench. We're about 1/4 of the way done.

By 15:00 the misty drizzle came full on with a severe weather warning issued. Despite this Kit and Saara came down for last nights pudding and to watch '300'. Saara was not impressed. By neither the violence nor the man boobs.

A stormy night meant I was up at 04:30 ensuring the awning and the man tent were still secure.

Friday 20/08/10

Drifted back to sleep after an early celestial performance of sheet lightning and far off thunder at 04:30. Was happily eating breakfast when Emma shouted, something about fire in the awning! Nearly broke my leg leaping out of the caravan onto the pallets to find my little 150w car inverter churning out a cloud of smoke (not wholly unexpected baring in mind its intended use). Took the battery to the barn for some topping up and surfed the net checking out inverters, emails, bank balance, then collected everyone's rubbish and recycling to take to the tip on our way to Llanelli and the nearest Maplin store.

Accidentally took the scenic route and on the return leg noticed the car was losing power in much the same way the Galant did the time we broke down at Lammas. This time however I'm pretty certain its the fuel filter after switching to Bio-Diesel. Ideally it needs a full service, but can't afford it right now...

Saturday 21/08/10

Another wet day. Useful in the way I find things that need doing that would otherwise have been forgotten or plain ignored. The slug population appears to have exploded! They get everywhere. Before, I was at ease with their existence. I accepted their presence and unless they were befouling something I held dear we enjoyed a harmonious relationship.

Not any more.

They're in my wellies. They're on the walls, they're on the awning zip ready to ambush you with a film of cold slime. They even hitch lifts in/on the car when you try and escape. Have dreamt up a new pastime and it contains just two ingredients. Slugs, and my nice new air rifle...

Aside from developing an irrational hatred of lower life forms, I also spent some time sorting out my overdue phone bill, watching the great Lee Evans, and typing up my diary onto the blog. My good deed of the day was in the form of helping another volunteer, an Icelandic chap who'd managed to puncture the tyre of his A reg VW camper on a screw. The trouble was, as we used the foot pump, it sank into the ground and sucked up mud, grit and water rendering it useless. I tried anyway...

Sunday 22/08/10

A break in the weather should have meant a window to catch up on some work outside, however Frances is being delivered back today and despite the warm sunshine not much has dried out properly.

My 'eco' washing machine...

To that end much of the day was spent doing very little aside from odd jobs until 15:00 when we were due to meet my parents in the village and guide them in.

Car unloaded, mostly filled with my brewing equipment, YEY! Followed by a coffee, a chat and a guided tour. Unfortunately my parents had to backtrack a fair way to stay at a travel lodge near my sister, so they only had an hour or so with us.

They were very impressed by all that's happening here and hopefully will come again and stay longer.

Monday 23/08/10

Beer recipe research. Am keen to find home brew recipes that don't require ingredients I don't have to hand I.e. malt extract, hops, barley etc. To that end most of the morning and early afternoon was spent on the internet in the 'clamp'.

The only distraction came in the form of two boys who'd found a jar of vintage 2007 sauerkraut and were eager to make a stink bomb using that and a crisp packet...

The only promising lead with recipes came from herbalbeers.com but aside from yarrow, I have no idea where to find mugwort or wormwood. Wormwood has psychotropic qualities so am most excited to hunt that bad boy down!

Am on taxiing duties so off to Whitland to collect Ayres after his business trip.

Was rather intrigued by what he had to say. How he's recently come to realise how in conversation, we all speak half truths. Not that we're dishonest but its also down to the questions we ask and are asked. One of these I personally have always had trouble with is "How are you?" And this is Ayres's point. Relative to what? "How are you?" - Well I'm not dead, so yes I might be considered medically sound. So the answer "I'm well" could be considered truthful...

Ayres's analogy was along the lines of observations or statements such as "It's cold isn't it" You might agree even though you perceive it to be warm. Again this can be measured but the question "Relative to what?" The Arctic? Hawaii? The Sun?!

That conversation has stuck with me and made me think.

I like that.

Tuesday 24/08/10

Our new 'Wendy' Wood burning stove

Wood burning stove arrived today just as the family we're helping left for the beach with some friends who are visiting.

Without help or instruction I set about ripping out the gas heater and punching a hole through the caravan wall for the flue. This is in spite of advice to go through the roof. The wisdom of this advice became apparent when I lit a small fire and got a thick stream of smoke billowing into my face. When Ayres returned he was exceedingly concerned with the whole set up which I already knew to be unsatisfactory, but to have a respected friend voice it really left me down about it.

That said, after dropping off Kit and Saara at Clunderwyn station and some fish & chips, I've had a rethink.

Patch up the damage and follow everyones advice. Go through the roof!

Wednesday 25/08/10

A trek to the nearest stove shop, a good 20 miles away. Explained the situation and came away £104 poorer. Bought cowling, flashing, a 'storm collar' and a 4" to 5" adapter. Wet and windy today so will wait for a lull before attempting anything. Sods law this evening has been bloody cold.

Thursday 26/08/10

Got the car booked in to get the fuel filter changed. Picked up a new filter on the way to the stove shop yesterday, so just a case of swapping it over. Attempted it myself but broke a neighbours filter strap in two places, so I heeded the gods warning and paid a professional.
The morning was spent against the clock and the weather, but now we have a properly installed and fully functioning wood burner.

Might need to buy a smaller kettle....

This evening was the opposite to last, was absolutely roasting! A fire truly does turn your shelter into a home.

Friday 27/08/10

Got a trailer load of logs on the way today. Should see us through until Spring. Not bad for £35! Went to get the cash this morning in order to be back to erect a dome. What type of dome, I wasn't told. All I was asked was to report to a certain field at 11:00 in order to help erect a dome for an hour. Went to the field at 11:00, no one there. No Dome. Hung around until 11:20. Not good as logs coming at 12:30. Eventually Paul came by around 13:00 after the logs had been delivered to ask me to go back as Will and Jam had arrived. Had got the kids building a log wall at the back of a tent, I doubt it'll take long before the novelty wears off.

The Diary And Path Of The Warless Warrior

Reported back to the field and worked until 17:45 building a "geo-dome with a Bedouin twist". Basically a dome with marquee canvas thrown over and pegged down. The dome was a '3 frequency' dome with plastic piping melted onto the ends of three different lengths of pole. Short Medium and Long. These were laid out in a specific pattern and then bolted together.

As this was done it pretty much built itself. So impressed am I, I reckon I'll build my own. Far better than a yurt or bender in my opinion.

The finished dome. Four hours after start.

The Diary And Path Of The Warless Warrior

Internal view of the geo dome

Close up of the geo dome joints.

Fran in the geo dome.

Saturday 28/08/10

Great to see people meeting, greeting and sharing.

The Diary And Path Of The Warless Warrior

A day of various activities ranging from tours to 'visioning' and guided meditation, to group work and lectures. All about how Lammas has come to fruition and how it can be replicated and reproduced. For me, its been fascinating to see the wide ranging backgrounds these like minded people are coming from. Some wish to retire to an eco community, others have land, others money, some with nothing but a burning and pressing desire to live off the land. Its a jigsaw puzzle that needs jigging so all the pieces fall into place, however, everyone is waiting for the other to take the leap, to create, so they can join.

Some of the most productive time has actually come from around the camp fire in the evening, where people have networked, explained their particular circumstances, and exchanged contact details and resolving to go further. Time will tell and separate the wheat from the chaff.

Sunday 29/08/10

The round up. I got the time slightly wrong so arrived a tad late. The group was arranged in a circle and giving their views on both the relevance and meaning of the weekend to them, and what they intended to do from now.

I was disappointed. By the group itself. As I said in the circle, it was quite apparent that the various circumstances of the individuals, the resources were all there to set up an eco village. Money, land, me the willing to volunteer etc But it was a jumbled jigsaw. A complete jigsaw that needed sorting. And therein lay the problem, each piece was looking to the other expecting someone to pick them up and put them in their place. This frustrated me no end.

All were unhappy with their current standing, yet none appeared willing to hold up the torch and get creating.

I loved an exercise Hoppi got us all to do. Everyone formed a circle, stood heel to toe with arms through the arms of the person in front and placed on their waist. We all sat down on the count of three. Each supported the weight of the other. Has to be done to be appreciated I think.
Walked up to Simon's and discussed my thoughts with Ayres and Simon,will talk to Paul tomorrow and hopefully get this dream manifested.

61

The Diary And Path Of The Warless Warrior

Didi, our host family's cat was most satisfied with our Wood Burner...

Very satisfied indeed

Monday 30/08/10

Pounding. Shovelling. Sifting. Dumping. This French drain is taking ages. Paul came to see me around 17:00 and we had a lengthy chat about my options with regards to buying land and replicating the Lammas model. All very encouraging, his pledge to support my efforts, most assuring. I just need to secure investment of probably £30k-£60k to get the ball rolling. Alot of money to someone without any! And its that alone that daunts me. All the rest has been done before. I guess so has the financial side...
Now my time or more specifically my thinking time, is consumed with these plans and ideas. Something will formulate but I know that even that will take time.

Tuesday 31/08/10

So far a week of fantastic weather. All good for building. Tinkering with the foundations of the timber post. The aim is to get them level, which will make life easier rather than being a necessity. Andy, another plot holder, has gone the other way and not bothered, electing to cut each timber. Steady progress.

Wednesday 01/09/10

Have exhausted our supply of the black slatey stuff, not too big a deal though, as we're going for a sunrise/sunset theme with the gravel. This means its back to the subsoil pile to sift out more of the light stuff. Along side this, more poles need stripping. Asked Ayres how much this project will cost. Probably a question he doesn't like to ask himself judging by the answer. I agree too. How can you put a price on shelter? What will be a home, albeit short term. What about the price of our labour? For the sake of argument an estimate was put around £2500. My reaction was, wow, that's expensive, but that's coming from someone without any money... If you think of the cost of conventional houses its nothing, Pocket change. You pay that much to solicitors alone. Not to mention tax/stamp duty. Really is food for thought.

Thursday 02/09/10

Dropped Fran off at her new school for her first day. Am happy and excited for her but hate the commitment to a routine albeit a 9-3. Just brings about memories of all we've left behind. After dropping her off and having had a tour of the school, it has left me questioning our aims and plan.

Its been quite apparent, in fact, from the outset, that these guys at Lammas are conventional folk like most others trying to reclaim the independence and freedom of our ancestors but without the sacred knowledge they held. As a result, they're going on instinct.

Whilst my intention is of touring and learning this knowledge, I'm reminded by nearly all the residents here that I have an enviable advantage over them. My youth. But I'm conscious this gift is gradually being revoked everyday. So I feel the need to find a way to buy land now and get cracking...

Frans new school. Outside play area complete with Wendy house!

Friday 03/09/10

10:00 meeting for a day trip! Have been invited to tag along for a visit to Brithdir Mawr for a little talk and demonstration about wood gasification and wood gasifiers. This is a subject I actually know a fair amount about. My ulterior motive was to see the set up and enquire about a few things as it was somewhere we'd considered joining after Lammas. Even more so when we'd heard they were looking for members!

Got to meet the fantastic Mr Tony Wrench, author of the book: Building A Low Impact Roundhouse. A real character and bloody nice bloke.

If it hadn't been for my thoughts the previous day, I would probably have said we'd be most likely to go there and live, however I'm torn. They all seem fantastic people. I suppose it depends on what my parents say and whether they can help me raise the cash on some land.

Saturday 04/09/10

Found myself out working until sundown. Am determined to finish off laying the gravel. Ayres was in Bath attending a funeral so it was just me. Without sounding like a hermit, I do enjoy working alone. Its not that I'm unsociable but with some good music in the headphones and a solid rhythm to your work I find I can really get things done without my mind and endless thoughts getting in my way.

Sunday 05/09/10

Attended what I believe is called a 'Blessing Way'. From what I understand a pagan ceremony where the community comes together to bless the way for a baby to enter this world and come to being. Only caught half of it as the first couple of hours was for the women to get together and do what women do best I imagine. The part us men were invited to involved singing, washing the mother-to-be's feet and offering two beads and a candle. This culminated with a ball of wool being woven around the circle, which was then cut and tied around each individuals wrist. Not to be removed, until mother and baby returned safely back from hospital.

Crap weather forecast, so may continue updating the blog. Have enjoyed reading Katy and Leanders blog. millpondpostcards.wordpress.com . Especially his humorous post about 'Munchman Flap Jacks'.

Monday 06/09/10

Rain. Kind of useful for everyone judging by the busyness of the clamp. There are no days off. Just different jobs that need doing.

Got a call around 13:00 from Ayres to ask for a lift back from Laurence's Garage due to his brake pads wearing out and grinding the discs. Was then time to pick up my truck load of kids, made interesting when Paul drew up exclaiming "Follow me!". Cool. Colin McRae mode, welsh rally stage. Doubt Monsieur McRae ever ran into a Freelander that was incapable of reversing... Was still a cool route which brings the school run into a loop. Have made a mental note to take more photos to liven up the blog. No excuse now digital photos are free. Borrowed 'Earth Sheltered Houses' - Rob Roy, from Simon D

Tuesday 07/09/10

It appears that leading a life independent of the marketplace (kind of) and everyday hustle and bustle comes at the cost of being out of sync with the rest of the busy world. Yet again, we took a trip to Cardigan only to find the banks and most of the shops shut. A bit ridiculous as the time hasn't changed. Now learnt the banks shut at 16:30 not 17:30 so I guess we can be forgiven somewhat. Its something more though.

One noticeable change has been when we pass an estate agents window. No longer are we looking for houses, but rather land. Emma says she now catches herself eyeing up other caravans!

I already find the volume of cars both intimidating and bloody annoying. As well as the fact I have to urinate in a designated place, and not behind a handy bush...just a personal grievance.

Am in the pathetic situation where I've been sent some cheques from my parents, but can't pay them in as my bank doesn't have a branch for miles. So I now have to send them back for my parents to pay in.

Aside from the above, had a chilled out day with the hosts cat on my lap. She just wouldn't move, and because I then couldn't lean forward when eating, she got a nice dusting.

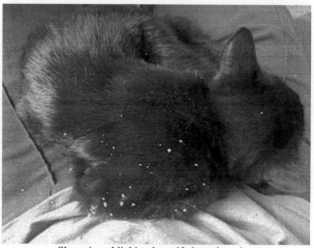

She enjoyed licking herself clean though...

Wednesday 08/09/10

Mist hanging in the valley.

The Diary And Path Of The Warless Warrior

Cool date! No work due to weather. Finished reading Earth-Sheltered Houses which I borrowed from Simon D. Interesting, but the author uses far too many modern materials and cop outs for my liking. The techniques are good though as well as the explanations and illustrations.

Ayres went off to collect his mother from Cardiff. Exciting stuff as she's coming from California!

Have been researching our options and looked more at Tinkers Bubble in Somerset. Seems like a definite possibility. Am mindful of the distance and the fact there are so many communities here in Wales that it would be silly to leave and come back. Would be useful to spend a rainy Saturday/Sunday visiting local places.

Thursday 09/09/10

End of French drain that will hopefully feed a pond

Where dark and light gravel meet to give Sunrise/Sunset effect.

Building site so far.

The Diary And Path Of The Warless Warrior

Was pleased and eager to be outside today. So much so, I was out past 20:00. Worked until I could barely see and a wood chip jumped up and smacked me square in the eyeball. Called it quits after that.

11 hours take the time spent on the school run and taking the children to the language centre.

Parents are invited to learn Welsh too to aid their child's learning. I completely agree, however couldn't help thinking "Yeah, but we won't be here that long..." So either we be here that long and commit to all the various initiatives, or we decide on what the hell we're doing with regards to the next place we're going. If its in England, then perhaps its not a productive use of our time. Although I'm all for not only us, but Frances learning Welsh, we have so many options and therein lies the problem.

Here are the options as I see them;

1) Leave in October for a place like Tinkers Bubble, where we can settle, or at least stay for the foreseeable future.

2) Stay at Lammas for as long as we're able, risking outstaying our welcome.

3) Buy land locally with the help of parents and replicating what Lammas have done. Either on our own or preferably with a group of others,

4) Buy land in England most likely a derelict farmstead and blazing a trail, again like Lammas. This would require substantial fund raising, but anything is possible.

5) Go WWOOFING

There are of course other factors to consider. Option 3 would be good if done close to Frans existing school which she very much enjoys.

There are 14 acres for sale for around £65000 with woodland, however that's a lot to manage on your own. Plus would only support 2 other families max. A very intimate community... The reality is that it would be further away. Slightly negating that option, but leads to yet another. Am so confused am going to talk to Paul tomorrow in the hope he can impart some wisdom from experience to aid my decision.

I guess this has all come about predominantly through an attack of conscience .

Our daughter has no control and is bound to follow us, her parents. I therefore feel honour and duty bound to ensure we still provide her with the best possible life that agrees with all of us. That will take compromise. But one thing I know for sure, the <u>only</u> definite I have is we will NOT return to 9-5's and 'the system' or the 'Matrix' as one guy called it.

Friday 10/09/10

A wet and windy millpond

Wet and windy today. Invented a game using my diary to test Emma's memory. She scared the hell out of me! She would zone in on an activity mentioned or memorable detail, refer to another day or date of fair proximity and count. After roughly ten seconds she'd get the day, not long after that she'd generally get the date too, although her counting would sometimes lead her astray. The incredibly embarrassing thing was that when she tested me I was way out. Not a clue. Even on days I had tested her on ten minutes prior!

I'm the first to admit my short term memory leaves a lot to be desired but boy did that shock me. And I'm only 25 years old. That's without abusing drugs, sure I enjoy my alcoholic beverages, but I'm hardly an ageing rock star!

Imagine what I'll be like when I'm 80 and senile. Will need more than this diary. Will probably have to draw a map just to know where my arse is! Best do that now before I forget....

Saturday 11/09/10

Yum Yums Sweets, Cardigan

Made another trek to Cardigan, rushed to get there before midday to catch the bank. Still too late as this branch obviously felt Monday-Friday were the only days their customers needed to administer their accounts.

Still, made the most of it by grabbing some sweets and an ice cream as well as some supplies from the supermarket. Had a very chilled out, but short evening as we went to bed at 20:45!

Sunday 12/09/10

The growing pile of stripped logs

Where the butchery takes place

The Diary And Path Of The Warless Warrior

The Diary And Path Of The Warless Warrior

In the morning we had a sit down chat with our host family. Was good to look forward and back on our time thus far. So good in fact, we have resolved to make it a monthly thing.

From there I took Frances, Davey and Bee to a birthday party in Llanfyrnach. Then wandered up to Pauls to gain some clarity. Amongst the many things we talked about, the bit of advice he gave that has been most useful right now is the saying "It is better to do nothing, than the wrong thing". To me, that says, chill out, hang tight and allow events and opportunities to unfold and present themselves.

In order to digest all that Paul had kindly imparted, I spent the rest of the afternoon stripping more poles under a surprisingly warm sky.

Ended the day around an open fire chatting to a select group who had gathered to honour another volunteers birthday.

Monday 13/09/10

The Circus?! Lions?Tigers?Bears? Nope - Katy and Leanders Roundhouse

Weather has turned. The next 48 hours are supposed to be high winds and rain. Despite this, I was amazed to see what appeared to be a circus 'Big Top' being assembled over on Katy and Leanders plot! In actual fact this massive red tarp was being spread over their roundhouse to allow them to finish the roofing.

Ayres and I waterproofed up to do some of our own building work, but decided to go and offer a hand whilst having a nose around.

We broke for lunch and I was busying myself cutting kindling, when for the second time so far I heard "Mike! FIRE!"

Fireman Mike was once again employed. This time to quench a pan of oil Emma had succeeded igniting. As I'm sure everyone knows, these can be potentially catastrophic if treated in the wrong way. Knowing that water would unleash a deadly napalm bomb I slid the lid over the pan in the hope of starving it of oxygen. This appeared to work until the lid, which was a size too big slid off. The pan then 'popped' and emitted a fireball and a jet of flame threatening to burn a hanging tea towel and the overhead cupboards.

With the lid carefully secured in place, the pan was taken outside where I was greeted by a train of excited children who had seen the flames and were all hoping to be the first to see our lives in carnage.

Sorry kids, I'm just too good.

I am of the opinion Emma secretly hates our new lifestyle and is progressively attempting different methods to destroy it! Will keep an eye on her I think.

Tuesday 14/09/10

Had an extremely vivid nightmare last night.

I was touring the countryside looking to buy some land, when I came across a dusty derelict farmstead. Next thing I knew we were living there and Emma was complaining of 'disturbances'. Before long she was being physically attacked by an unseen force. I remember being absolutely enraged by this and doing battle with this thing,. Absolute to the death fighting, but the more angry I was, the stronger the force I was fighting became. Realising this, I consciously forced myself to risk calming, and luckily it worked, the threat melting away.

Suspecting another ambush and far from convinced I had defeated it, I sought the advice of Emma's mum to help protect and rid us of this ethereal menace. She asked for the help of the angels and I was dressed in a silver breastplate and armour. Whilst I could see it and felt it strapped on, it wasn't physical and couldn't be seen by others. Call it spiritual armour. I was assured, should the demon strike again, I would remain unharmed.

Life quietened down and I arranged to talk to the estate agent to learn some of the properties history. I was to expect a visit that day. Very shortly after, a woman arrived. We shook hands and she handed me the sales particulars. As I glanced them over my eye was drawn to an interior shot, where in the mirror I saw the cloudy reflection of a female. I started to point this out to the woman as a poor photographers error, when I further noticed a blur of orange in the corner of the photograph. As though in fact the camera had caught the spirit of a lady looking into the mirror, perhaps doing her make up. Reinspecting the image in the mirror, the face was horribly distorted conveying anger and hatred. It was clear this spirit was that of a former owner who was distressed at our presence.

I handed the particulars back to the woman and began to tell her what I'd seen, but stopped. Her hair was ginger. Orange. Her coat a reddy tartan. It was her... At lightning speed the realisation set in. "You're her". She gave a wry knowing smile. Before I could ask "But how come I can see you?", the penny dropped. My mind told me. I'm dead. "You killed me" was all I could utter and her smile spread as she lifted her hand and revealed how she had done it. Hidden between her fingers, was a small ball headed pin. Dipped in poison, all it needed, was for me to offer the unprotected flesh of my palm and my life was taken...

Reads like a crap Hollywood horror I know, but boy did it scare the hell out of me... not too badly considering I went on to dream I found my former headmistress living in a yurt behind a training hospital and medical research centre in Tipi Valley. Weird

Night time entertainment over, I took the tiddlywinks to school, went to Cardigan AGAIN. This time caught the Bank. Enjoyed an egg roll, cheesy chips and a coffee before returning home.

Posed for a Lammas group photo, still feel weird about that sort of thing, as I'm rather mindful we're just volunteers.

The Diary And Path Of The Warless Warrior

The Singer sewing machine I rescued whilst working on the bins.

Played with the rescued Singer sewing machine, the first time its been used since we've had it. Was pretty fun using all the weird and wonderful attachments, but best left to Emma I think until I can work out how she threaded the damn thing.

Sun suddenly decided to show after a grey day so nearly all of us grabbed the opportunity to step outside. Spent the evening reading my new books that arrived today bought with birthday money.

One is RSPB Pocket Nature Wildlife of Britain . The other is Practical Self Sufficiency .

The Wildlife book I bought because of the fact it has everything from trees to plants to mammals to flies and beetles matched to excellent clear photographs.

The self sufficiency guide, I bought because it actually <u>shows</u> you how to build, make, brew all the stuff other books just say you can do. Really chuffed.

Wednesday 15/09/10

Rammed earth tyres. The agenda for the day. 6 Volunteers arrived last night from Scotland! A 12 hour drive. An amazing mix of stories. South Africans, Hawaiians, English, American, German. Incredible group. As I got chatting, it transpired they came from a community called Culdees I'd read about a couple of nights prior and had been so drawn to, it was a place I thought we could go to after Lammas.

Worked on the site from 10:00 - 13:30 then went back for half an hour until 15:00 as I had to collect the kids and did another hour or so after that. Was pooped by the end.

On a tea break, Simon took the visitors to his place.

Our first completed tyre...

Quite a few more to go!

Not bad progress. Two more courses to go.

Thursday 16/09/10

Had to engage the brain early today as a school run 'system' was changed. a pre breakfast text flurry ensured the tiddlywinks were covered.

More rammed earth tyres with the guys from Culdees.

Weather has been on and off, but for the most part sunny and dry. Am conscious that the sun is now setting around 19:30 and not rising until 06:56. With the days closing in, I am also keeping a weather eye, as inevitably our productive days will diminish.

Although I'm committed to seeing as much of the building done as I can, I'm also aware the travel urge is creeping in. Is it because of the routine I ask myself? Is this an underlying subconscious thing?

The Diary And Path Of The Warless Warrior

How in control of my life and more importantly, my mind, am I?

Friday 17/09/10

Got a call asking if I'd be up for some paid work Monday. Has led me to try and find a way of bringing in some steady cash without the strings of conventional employment.

Unsurprisingly, the viable options appear rather limited. Online paid surveys? Doubt they're 'easy' money. In order to bring in anything acceptable I'd imagine you'd need to sit in front of a machine for 8 hours a day 5 days a week as your eyesight faded and brain liquefied.

Could write a guide perhaps? Do I have the patience or even know anything of use? I like the idea of perhaps writing some short e-books. Cheap. Short. Am not out to make millions, Just enough so our expenses don't completely drain our accounts each month... That said, isn't that what the whole world is trying to do?

Saturday 18/09/10

Attended Fran's School Fête Was a nice little village affair with various simple amusements including a dunk tank!

I managed to become almost obsessed with the "Guess The Weight Of The Pumpkin" so much so, I snuck a photo of the list of guesses and tried to gain the upper hand using the law of averages. This led me to the answer of 15.56811 kg however when I eventually returned to enter my super accurate 'guess' I was devastated to see more guesses. Still, I couldn't back out, so I paid for my guess and hung around until the very end. By which time there were 23 more guesses! One more. I took another clandestine photo and scuttled off with the vain hope my average had only been minutely changed. No such luck. The new average was a massive 4kg over the previous! Damn you Derren Brown. Where are you when I need you!?

It was no longer, indeed was never, about the prize. Simply ensuring that maths was still a constant in my life. If that bloody pumpkin doesn't weigh 19.27023kgs or even better, my earlier guess of 15.56811kgs, I will simply be distraught.

The Diary And Path Of The Warless Warrior

Frans School

The Dunk Tank, which must have taken ALOT of money that day!

The Diary And Path Of The Warless Warrior

Good old tug of war

Face painting kept Em busy...

Monday 20/09/10

Up early to gather some kit for todays work. Charlie appeared at 08:50 and we set off for Willow's Forest. What greeted me was an incredible 325 acres of Douglas and Norwegian Fir set across a valley.

The Diary And Path Of The Warless Warrior

Our task was to strip the bark off some 200 2m long sections. For this we had a tractor attachment. This machine was basically 2 cogs and a cheese grater. The log was fed in and gripped in a death roll as an alligator might an antelope, then grated at an obscene speed. Was a horrific and fascinating sight. In the first hour it devoured 57 lengths!

Pretty back breaking work and was glad when 17:15 rolled around. 7.5 hours well, 8 hours minus half an hour break.

Got a text to say there was football going on. Was torn. I was pooped, but at the same time liked the sound of a kick around, even if it made tomorrows labour even more painful.

I decided to go as I felt if I didn't on the basis of work the next day, and being tired from todays toil, I'd be living to work and not the other way around.

We left in Ayres' car and were delayed as one of the guys was a volunteer who needed to erect his tent whilst it was still light. On the way we met a large 4x4 coming the other way driven by a woman who looked far from confident at passing in such a narrow lane. Therefore Ayres had to squeeze further in than was necessary. She passed fine, but as we pulled back out BANG! Ayres gouged out a chunk of his front tyre side wall and a large part of the alloy rim. Not good. He dropped us back, understandably rather pissed off and we took my truck. As a result we only played 30-45 mins but that suited me just fine. Feel sorry for Ayres though...

Tuesday 21/09/10

The Diary And Path Of The Warless Warrior

All this machinery means just one man can maintain and harvest this huge forest.

Round two. One man down, so with Charlie and Ritchie on the receiving end I fed the logs through on my own. Right up until 14:30 when the machine broke down. Left at 16:45 making it a 7 hour day. Stopped off at Glandy Cross to pick up some bits after visiting Charlies partner, who, incidentally is working on a farm due to be taken over and run by the owners of Ruskin Mill in Stroud!

Have been offered another day, possibly two of work, but I have turned it down. Partly will welcome the change of pace, plus helping Ayres on the building, is what I'm here to do and this week we have some volunteers to help.

Plus I am fully aware that should I start bringing in money, we'll find things to spend it on. Am currently enjoying not spending by virtue of not having anything to spend!

Wednesday 22/09/10

This week being a volunteer week at Lammas, we have 2 extra pairs of hands. Ayres has been making use of them with a variety of tasks being set. Alot is needing doing. Bales need moving, trees need staking, beds need resurrecting, as well as poles needing stripping (by hand!). With today being the first day of autumn, there was certainly an autumnal feel I.e. the weather was shit. Whilst I agree with the saying "There is no such thing as bad weather, just bad clothing" I still prefer to keep dry. Water proofs are ok, but with hot work they soon lose their benefit as you overheat and become drenched in sweat.

Am becoming concerned about our battery. The controller is now reading between 12 and 11.3 volts. Not sure how to gauge the state of the battery from that, but I guess its low as up until now its rarely dipped below 12 volts. I now have a choice. Spend my earnings on a service on the car, ensuring mobility, or purchase an auxiliary form of electricity generation in the form of a 50w wind turbine.

Being that I <u>could</u> just charge the battery in the barn off mains, I guess logic would dictate I opt for a service. But a service is just so boring...

Thursday 23/09/10

Another pair of volunteers. Put them to work stripping logs but also made full use of having 4 people by using a bearer system to carry poles from a pile at the bottom of the plot. Just as well too as they are predominantly of a larger diameter of Japanese and European larch. After a conversation with one of yesterdays volunteers, Ayres has now decided to extend the building by putting an indoor/outdoor space to the front.

The theory being this would serve to capture and store more natural heat as well as promote natural convection. There was also talk of underfloor heating using the back boiler he has attached to another wood burner.

Will be interesting to see whether this indeed happens and how it would come together.

Another evolution in the plan.

A volunteer from... No prizes for guessing.... that's right, Tipi Valley!

Gappy loses another tooth.

Saturday 25/09/10

Took a walk up the top past Simon D's. A beautiful spot apparently owned by a Belgian couple. Rather selfishly if you ask me. You could fit another Lammas again up there. Plus, it kind of goes against the eco principles being that they've bought 28 acres. The common notion is that roughly 5 acres is enough to support one family. Anything more than that cannot realistically be managed by one household without the employment of mechanical assistance.

Still. We wandered down through the woodland coming across a wonderful variety of wild flowers and wild produce. Mistook an Earthball for a Puffball! Well, only for a split second. After squeezing the top I revealed a chamber of spores and with the help of my new RSPB Wildlife Of Britain book, I learnt the differences and the fact the Earthball is in fact poisonous.

The Diary And Path Of The Warless Warrior

After showering at Ayres' I found myself reading a great little book called Keep Calm and Carry On: Good Advice for Hard Times. The inspiration for which, was the third of three wartime posters, the last of which was never issued. This final poster with this simple message, was to be plastered in tube stations should the Germans have invaded. I love its Britishness.

Tried to watch Yes Man but our charge controller put an end to that with a low battery warning. Had a hunch the shorter days were taking their toll on our solar panels. Had an idea to hook up a bicycle to a washing machine motor and a rectifier. Half to an hour a day on that should provide all of our electrical power...In theory.

The Diary And Path Of The Warless Warrior

The Diary And Path Of The Warless Warrior

The Diary And Path Of The Warless Warrior

Cherries? I hope so as I ate one...

Sunday 26/09/10

Took a stroll around with Em and Fran. Bumped into Paul W and a couple of chaps from The Guardian. Those guys don't seem to be able to get enough of this place. I swear they have done at least two articles already.

Ended up with serious land envy. Seeing all the tracts and imagining what I'd do with it. Ridiculous, I know when you haven't a penny to your name. I guess squatting is the only option.

The Diary And Path Of The Warless Warrior

A visit from Didi - or as I prefer to call her Iddy Biddy Diddy Kitty. Her full name.

Tuesday 28/09/10

Simon D had asked me on Sunday whether I was up for some work Tuesday, Wednesday and Thursday. Persuaded Emma to join me. Bit of a mistake. Ended up stripping logs instead of plastering boards with lime - oops. Don't think she'll risk tomorrow.

Had an emotional outburst from Fran last night regarding school. Turns out she's now feeling excluded by the language barrier and being physically and verbally bullied. Ideally she wants to go back to her previous school. Ironically just that morning we'd informed her old school of her new one. Had we not, it would have probably been easy to get her back in, as she was still on the books.

With that in mind, I think it is quite likely we will return at least to England. If only to minimise the impact of this new life on Frans schooling.

The roofing continues.

Wednesday 29/09/10

Lime plaster. But first a punishing session with the gas powered nail gun. My task was to nail thin strips of wood to the panels creating a rough surface for the plaster to adhere to. Punishing, as I failed to notice the heat of the gun burnt the first layers of skin off my thumb!

Next job, plastering. The mix was something like two parts lime 1 part sand? some horse hair in there too... good messy fun to a background of reggae tunes.

Simon D mixing it up

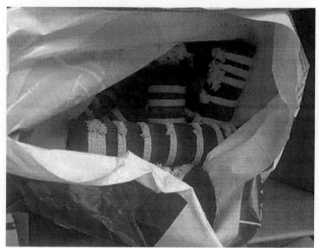

A bag of horse hair

The panels to be plastered.

The 'factory' floor.

Thursday 30/09/10

More plastering, but only two hours today.

Tasted my hawthorn brew today. Definitely alcoholic but rather watery. Noticed the other day the scum that has been sitting on the top had developed a few patches of green mould. Rather hastily grabbed the sieve and scooped that out. Spoke to fellow brewer Simon D about it and to my surprise he told me he'd brewed a damson recipe that had stipulated to wait until such a mould appeared. Don't think I'll leave it much longer before bottling. Am still undecided whether to treat it as a wine and rack it off into demijohns, or add 80g/3oz of sugar for carbonation and bottle like a beer. Am leaning towards wine due to the high alcohol taste and wateriness.

My Eco-Dishwasher being harassed by the cat.

The bales go on Katy and Leanders Roof.

Friday 01/10/10

The battery is dead. The remedy, electrical resurrection. Drove it over to plug it in to the mains. What I didn't take into account was how long it would take to charge a 110 amp hour battery. A 'fast' charge puts in 6 amps an hour, taking 18 hours. Preferable to a normal charge that would only put in 2 amps and therefore take 55 hours! A pain as it means not only relying solely on our two cheap hurricane lanterns, but also Fran will have to go without her usual 'movie night' tonight.

Rang the mechanic, Lawrence, to book the car in for a service. Due to the fact I haven't a clue when it was last done, everything needs doing. The minimum damage - £400! Have arranged to drop it to him Tuesday morning. The justification in my mind is a) this should lower the risk of breaking down in the middle of nowhere b) once done, most areas won't need replacing for two years or so, I hope.

115

Our celestial power station just ain't juicing the panels like it did...

Saturday 02/10/10

Picked up the battery after its 18 hours of resurrection. Forgot today was a 'Community Engagement' day. The intention of this was to invite the locals to see the progress and answer their questions. A bit difficult when apparently hardly any of the large number of visitors were local. Didn't particularly want to stick around with all the people about so we took a day trip to Cardigan instead.
Whilst there I picked up six of those LED stick on lights, a huge adjustable spanner, 3 books for Frances (Classic Ghost Stories, Children's Encyclopedia and British Wildlife) and some food. Wanted Fish and Chips but they were shut
With the battery back online we settled down to watch one of Frans new films 'The Ant Bully' Pretty entertaining, certainly passed the time.

Sunday 03/10/10

Finally bottled the Hawthorn Brew. Double checked it had finally finished fermenting with the hydrometer. This also gave me the ABV. (OG - FG) x 7.46 + .5 = SG in this instance (1026 - 1000) x 7.46 + .5 = 3.98% ABV.

Gave away four bottles. Two to Katy and Leander and two to Ayres. Barrelled the rest. From the small amount I sampled, what started as a mash that resembled, and smelt like vomit, it appears to have transformed into a pleasant hedgerow tonic.

Monday 04/10/10

Joined Ayres, Simon (the tree surgeon) and volunteer for the week, Helen, in the woods to collect firewood felled a while ago. Had an interesting time trying to turn a land rover and large trailer around on a narrow woodland trail, overlooking a deadly drop...

Football night. This time Ayres joined us. He likened the new pace of the indoor game to watching a Japanese game show. "Blah blah blah Brother. Blah blah blah October". I know what he means. With the ball bouncing around you can find yourself a spectator, but for a frantic few seconds pitched headlong into the thick of the action.

He won't be returning until April when the guys play outdoors again.

I on the other hand have been asked to play in the 5 a side league...

View through the trees.

The building pad being reclaimed by nature after a spell of inactivity.

Tuesday 05/10/10

Paul W invited me up to his for a quick chat. Turns out he wanted to give me the heads up on a really good opportunity to buy some land nearby. We walked over to check it out and it is gorgeous.

We were so taken by it we rang both our families to see if they could help us out. They said no. Couldn't help but feel disappointed. Especially as it is likely to be snapped up by the end of the week.

I guess we'll have to do it on our own, which I respect. I don't want debt, and up until recently, people saved, not borrowed. Since the financial meltdown, it would appear to be our only option. That and wait until the very people we wish to share our experience with, our parents, croak. An unhappy and morbid thought.

The Diary And Path Of The Warless Warrior

Emma using the time honoured method of
swinging your arms to survey a potential building site.

Thursday 07/10/10

Was pre-warned yesterday to set my alarm in order to get up and be ready for work at the ungodly hour of 09:00. This was a shock to the system, as we have gotten used to sleeping our fill each night and rising when we feel we're ready. This is normally around 09:00 and breakfasted by 10:00. Between the numerous and repeated groans and protests from Emma, I joked about how awful a life it would be if you had to do this everyday. The hardship of only being allowed to wake when you feel like it, just two days of the week. Then it hit me. As perverse as it sounds, I believe alot of truth was said in my jests. No other creature on earth forces itself to wake at a set time each day. No other animal in nature forces itself to work when ill. In fact, I dare say, there are very few other beings that continually force themselves to engage in an activity they do not want to do 5 out of 7 days a week, then kid themselves they are happy doing it and that's "just life".

Today was about milling timber. Ayres had booked Adrian and his 'Wood-Mizer' and we processed 13 or so logs. What surprised me was how little usable timber is milled from one tree.

Got a good amount of practice reversing with a trailer which is invaluable when you own a caravan.

By 17:30 I was very tired. Slept soundly in the knowledge no alarm waited to disturb my restful slumber.

Wednesday 13/10/10

Have returned to see friends and family for a week. The whole trip was nearly scrapped after Didi, our friendly neighbourhood kitten, staged a 'sit on' protest.

So far we've crammed in the TV, DVD's and internet but are sorely missing the countryside.
Appreciated, I'm on holiday so to speak, but I have an overwhelming feeling of not being able to do anything. A very painful memory. When you're living in a Barratt box modern home with bugger all land, what can you do? No, or very little garden is great for people who are at work all day busy paying bills.

Night time has literally illuminated something I sorely miss and will prevent me ever returning to live in or near a major city or town.

I miss the stars.

Caught a shot of carpets going over the bales before we left.

Thursday 19/10/10

The Diary And Path Of The Warless Warrior

The Diary And Path Of The Warless Warrior

The Diary And Path Of The Warless Warrior

Arrived back at Lammas at 20:00 Sunday evening. Was a fantastic feeling. Definitely one of returning home, which says alot to me.

Monday morning I was thrown straight back into the mix for what turned out to be a phenomenal days work. It was the stage I have been looking forward to. A stage that gives this build the visual and psychological leap forward into tangibility and manifestation.

The timber framework at this point resembles a henge.

Had great fun playing with a tripod I made with Rudolph.

Although we were only gone from Lammas a week, there appears to have been an explosion of progress and activity in our absence. Andy and Jane's turf roof is on, as is Katy and Leander's, Paul and Hoppi have also finished roofing and waterproofing their barn. And as of Monday morning Simon D has begun work on his workshop and already made substantial headway.

Another leap has come in the form of long term volunteers. We now have 6 more people here, three of whom arrived during the week we were away.

This, and the aforementioned changes have resulted in me feeling rather out of touch, if not left behind somewhat. Am hoping in a couple of days I'll have settled back in and caught up.

Ayres and Marianne had a visit from the BBC today. Was rather surreal really.

Woke up around 08:30/09:00 and stepped outside looking nicely dishevelled, to be greeted by a camera and sound crew filming Ayres chopping firewood. As sods law would have it, our awning door was right behind Ayres and bang in the middle of their shot. Will no doubt make an entertaining out-take!

We looked after the children whilst the crew interviewed Ayres and Marianne, I think on the subject of money and their relationship to it.

Don't think I can imagine a more mundane 15 minutes of fame quite frankly.

If they had asked me about my relationship to money, I'd have to say it is very much akin to a one night stand, as illustrated by my trip to the petrol station today. Can't help feeling like I've been screwed.

Late afternoon I took to wandering and delivering bottles of my hawthorn brew. Am very glad I did. Was humbled and grateful to meet a chap called Dave, who it transpired was a reader of my blog and gave some very kind feedback. A very very big thank you Dave! Hope to see you back here again soon!

Wednesday 20/10/10

The Diary And Path Of The Warless Warrior

The Diary And Path Of The Warless Warrior

Awake all night pretty much. Enjoyed chatting to Rob, a newcomer who's volunteering with Andy and Jane. We talked until just gone 23:00 sitting inside his rather spacious yurt. Considering it is him on his own in there, it is by comparison to most, positively palatial. Just as I finally clambered over Emma into bed and settled, the heavens machine gunned the roof of our caravan with hailstones. This continued sporadically over the course of the night, the volleys coming in varying degrees of severity.

At 04:00 Fran awoke from a nightmare and complained of cold. With only a handful of kindling to revive the burner, I dressed, and filled a bucket with kindling and logs. This took me a pleasantly meditative half an hour, after which I made us all a hot chocolate.

Another attempt to sleep was sabotaged by my over active and now awake brain and conscience. I was filled with worry and concern for another volunteer, Alexandra. For what must be a month now, she has battled an ongoing saga of trying to get a wood burner in her otherwise heatless caravan. Actually, that isn't entirely accurate. She has a gas heater. That leaks. So I suppose she has the option to fall asleep cosy and warm, never to awake. Anxious to ensure this is resolved ASAP for the sake of her health and general well being. I text volunteer coordinator, Hoppi, my concerns at 05:54. To my amazement, she text back almost immediately! We ended up

141

having a really productive dawn meeting ensuring agreements are amended to prevent the situation arising in the future, as well as putting a plan in place to sort this situation as quickly as possible.

Breakfast, then que my next walkabout. Checked in with Katy and Leander, very impressed by both their progress and ingenuity. For vents to insert through their stonewalling; plastic tubing and mesh cannibalised from a sieve. For roof drainage; plastic pipe, pond liner, inserted with marker pen tops shoved down to secure the liner in place. Further more, it is visibly apparent that the roof drainage is effective and fit for purpose. Well done Katy for that burst of inspiration!
From Katy and Leanders I meandered up to Kits plot where I was promptly press ganged into sorting a pile of bricks into grades and stacking them onto pallets. That took me up to lunch time.

14:30 reconvened with Hoppi and joined by Andy. Have offered myself and Emma to be named contacts should other long term volunteers need any help and support. This I hope, along with monthly meetings, serve to nip any issues in the bud, before they have a chance to blossom into full blown problems. Spent the rest of this very very cold day on idle setting. Am rather exhausted to say the least.

Friday 22/10/10

The Diary And Path Of The Warless Warrior

The Diary And Path Of The Warless Warrior

I believe the day started with a breakfast bowl containing the last of the Weetos purchased during our visit to Stroud. This was followed some time later by the departure of our host family as they themselves visit the town in which they previously resided for the next seven days.

Up until 15:55 I was employed in the service of Kit. My duties included preparation for the digging of the foundations of his build, transportation of timber out of the barn and up to his plot, and very much later, assisting with the marking of the proposed trenches set to be dug at 10:00 Friday morning.

Before his departure Ayres had requested I attend an auction of tools, set to take place in the barn at 16:00, in his stead. The tool he had his eye on and wished for me to bid on in his place, was a fine looking Adze.

Quite what this tool is intended for, I do not at this moment in time know, but Simon obviously did and outbid me. The irony is, Ayres will inevitably end up borrowing it! Over the course of the next hour and a half I got embroiled in numerous bidding wars and came away substantially poorer and the owner of various tools I do not yet have a need for. Delivered a keg of home brewed bitter to Melissa in lieu of her birthday party on Saturday, then it was up to Kits plot to mark his building pad by the light of my trucks headlights.

Another restless night which forced me to Ayres' static caravan for some midnight green building research.

Friday morning I met Kit on his plot at the arranged time of 09:30. A few cigarettes and two coffees later the excavator arrived. Not at 10:00 but more like 11:00. Once we got started and stuck in, we worked hard until we broke for lunch at 13:00. Justin, a volunteer on Nigel's plot and yesterdays auctioneer, borrowed my truck to tow a trailer to carry sand. Due to odd jobs springing up, they had not finished with it at 15:00 as agreed. This made me late leaving for Cardigan and cost me brownie points with my dear Lady Love.

Film night tonight. 'A Series Of Unfortunate Events', then bed. God Bless it.

Saturday 23/10/10

Rubble trench laid with reclaimed bricks.

The Diary And Path Of The Warless Warrior

I am officially declaring last night as the last sleeping starkas night for this year. Why? Because its been bloody cold recently, and despite being a 'hot' sleeper I've managed to contract a phlegmy cough and a runny nose. From this day or rather night, forth I shall include donning a t-shirt in my bedtime routine. Another reason for mentioning this, is not only is it useful to note, but I would hate to think there were men out there, naked and shivering each night because no one had taken the time to tell them it is now too cold. There. Conscience cleansed.

Took a stroll up to Kits at 13:00 to find him in the dark, reading a book and suffering from a monster hangover. Left him to it. On my return, I observed that wonderful sight synonymous with country living and often pictured in school history textbooks. A human chain unloading 200 odd bales of straw. My feeble excuse of merely observing and recording failed to hold water and I was swiftly press ganged into the ranks.

But around here, if we work hard, we play hard. So at 16:00 the gathering to celebrate Melissa's 40th Birthday began to muster, and around 23:00 an exhausted and beer filled me, made and devoured an egg sandwich, and gladly clambered into his bed. Leaving on his shirt.

Thursday 28/10/10

Foolishly, I made a hand print in the grime from the paraffin lanterns, and was made to clean it. So being immature, I only cleaned my side...

Emma using our rescued hand powered Singer sewing machine for the first time.
The cold called for some heavy curtains that made a huge difference.

The Diary And Path Of The Warless Warrior

Kit having a quick whack by himself.

Ironically, since Ayres and family departed last week I have been the busiest I've probably been since my arrival. Finished Kits foundations yesterday after a full days graft. He'll now be leaving the rammed stone to wash and settle naturally over the coming week. Well timed too as Ayres returned around 16:00 yesterday.

Monday nights football was very productive, had a fantastic game following which it transpired the oppositions goalkeeper was none other than the owner of the farm next door. This prompted me to suggest us volunteers trooping down to his to help out. This I feel, will give us the husbandry and livestock experience currently lacking at this phase of Lammas' development. Would also help with public relations. Nice and neighbourly and all that.

Tonight we have a gathering of volunteers down at the local pub. I believe its intention is to be a relaxed, informal affair where we can raise and discuss topics of varying importance. Might turn out that the term 'piss up' becomes more accurate...

Saturday 30/10/10

Simon D's latest creation, a workshop.

The Diary And Path Of The Warless Warrior

Kits walled garden. A bit waterlogged.

The Diary And Path Of The Warless Warrior

With an influx of volunteers, this place became quite a work camp. Ayres and I concentrated on building and seating the first cross beam of the henge. Took all day to cut and fine tune two joints. Others were employed looking after the many children, digging a foundation trench for a shed and transporting top soil into raised beds where garlic will be grown.

After lunch a large ominous cloud rolled in and pelted us with rain and hail. In the poly tunnel the sound was magnified making conversation nigh on impossible. Have found myself feeling lethargic and drained. I still haven't shaken my cough. Have resolved to take it easy tomorrow in order to knock this on the head.

Thursday 04/11/10

The Diary And Path Of The Warless Warrior

The Diary And Path Of The Warless Warrior

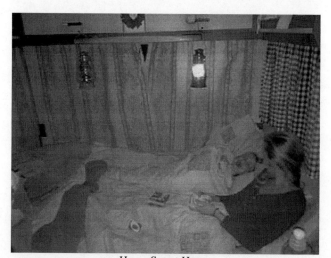

Home Sweet Home

Since Saturday, I've been engaged in quite an assortment of tasks and activities. Helped cut and raise another cross beam on the henge. Its becoming clear that by the way we're doing it we'll be averaging one a day.

Tuesday saw us take a trip to Llanmadoc on the Gower peninsula outside Swansea. Whilst Kit and I packed his things into our truck and his trailer, Em and Fran picked apples and went for a walk. Despite the poor weather and overcast sky some of the scenes around there are most impressive.

We didn't arrive back until late so it wasn't until Wednesday morning that I noticed another cross member had been cut and raised in my absence.

Booked the car in to have a sidelight replaced, as well as have the electrics looked at after the batteries died last Monday night at football. So at 15:00 Wednesday afternoon, kit and I trundled off to Bwlchygroes. We didn't leave there until 16:55 and I'd been told I needed two new batteries. By 17:30 my meagre savings had been wiped out and I was £125.04 poorer. But the proud owner of two Numax Premium Silver 68ah batteries. Forgetting the £80 to fill the tank each time, this car has now cost me in excess of £750 in maintenance this year. A stark reminder of how big a liability these machines are. I could comfort myself in the thought that at least the batteries should be good for the next 5 years, but I liked having savings.

Friday 05/11/10

"Remember, remember the fifth of November, gunpowder, treason and plot. I see no reason, why gunpowder treason, should ever be forgot..."

I'm sure there is some deep meaning and parallel between the events of 1605 and what we are doing here today.

If one looks past the 36 barrels of gunpowder and what would be termed today simply as terrorism, one could possibly recognise both of us are hoping our actions will result in a radical change in society and current accepted methods and beliefs.

But for tonight, Guy Fawkes will return and the inner pyromaniac in all of us that he represents, will rejoice in burning and blowing shit up.

Monday 08/11/10

A game changing day. Emma had been feeling 'off' for the past few days.
Being past her sell by date and having inclinations towards incubation, we
took a trip to Crymych at 09:00 to get a pregnancy test.

The result was "Pregnant 3+"

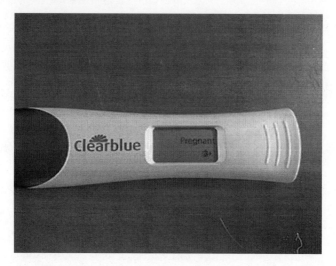

A flurry of text messaging to random folk and an emergency meeting with
Ayres and Marianne. Frances took it upon herself to spill the beans before we
had a chance, and subsequently faced Emma's wrath.

A serious talk about the whole thing brought forth many ideas and potential
possibilities, the main one being to consult Paul and Hoppi. Paul knows the
ins and outs of both the planning and the leasehold agreements. therefore is
it even feasible for Lammas to absorb another family? It was only designed
and got permission for nine. We are looking for long term stability along the
lines of 2-5 years. This being the case, I simply don't feel Lammas is the
place. We do have an offer from another plot holder that would grants us
that, but to accept this would fly in the face of rules and policies. As always
one can manipulate such things but its definitely not a practice I wish to
engage in.

The Diary And Path Of The Warless Warrior

Here's the truth. We have no right to be here. To remain beyond Spring would tread on toes and upset people we've come to hold dear, and whose generosity has known no bounds thus far. Once more I am writing lists of options and at this moment in time, here they are;

1) Remain in or near Lammas. kits plot verbally guaranteed for two years. Possibility of more living space in the form of a static caravan. Other options and possibilities could evolve from this, but mindful of aforementioned factors.

2) Tipi Valley. Plenty of experience in residents re. Home births. Poor access to lower valley - emergencies. Ideally a Yurt to live in. Would entail logistics moving our life and home. Would be guaranteed for as many years as we'd require. We have visited and know people there.

3) Join a different community. Tinkers Bubble? Would be an unknown unless we used the time we have to make prior visits.

4) Go back home. Ideally rent/buy/get permission to reside on land in a caravan or yurt. Alot of unknowns.

5) Sell out and return to the system be it in Wales or back in Stroud. For me, the least desirable of all. Benefits could be seen as wide and numerous, but at a vast cost spiritually, morally and financially.

6) Squat on land. Extremely unstable. Many variables and unknowns. One important disadvantage, we'd be on our own...

7) Buy our own land. a big ask financially. would require major help from family. Unlikely in probability and unlikely to be finalised in time frame.

8) Wait and see...

Listing is useful. But inconclusive. Will follow option 8 for now. I feel immense pressure to properly lead this family, and lead it well. Its bewildering and overwhelming now. One realisation is that, at this point, nothing has changed. The considerations, yes. But as those who've read previously will know, the options haven't really changed. I've created a mental pressure that has left my stomach knotted and mind exhausted.

If anything, this news has become a catalyst.

The Diary And Path Of The Warless Warrior

Will have to ransom this grandchild if money is the answer.

Hopefully a good hour of football tonight will help clear this over active brain.

Barley shoots growing from a bale weighting our awning down.

The Diary And Path Of The Warless Warrior

The Diary And Path Of The Warless Warrior

177

The Path Of The Warless Warrior

09/11/10 - 24/04/11

A Book Of The Blog
www.1nomad.blogspot.com

by Mike Jones

The Diary And Path Of The Warless Warrior

With infinite love and respect to all those at Lammas.
Thank you and Bless you, the lessons you have taught me will
never be forgotten.

"I went into the woods because I wished to live deliberately, to front only the essential facts of life, and see if I could not learn what it had to teach, and not, when I came to die, discover that I had not lived."

— Henry David Thoreau,
Walden; Or Life In The Woods

Tuesday 09/11/10

10:00 I saw various faces walking past the caravan to Ayres'. It wasn't until the third person that I remembered today was a committee meeting that I had resolved to attend. Those that also attended included Jane (Plot 1), Katy (Plot 2), Ayres and Marianne (Plot 3), Jude (Plot 4), Myself, Kit, Paul W, Simon D, Justin (Volunteer) and Nigel.

The matter consumed 4 hours related to one incident. This incident however had many far reaching ramifications. These areas encompassed - law, policy and procedure, professional and personal conduct/misconduct, Lammas as an organisation, Lammas as Tir Y Gafel village and many other issues. I say it consumed 4 hours, in reality it will probably be more after reviews have taken place and been discussed at the next meeting.

By 15:00 I was feeling both mentally and physically drained. But what a valuable experience.

The question that could be asked by residents is "Why did Mike attend?" The answer to that is this.

Many people that visit Tir Y Gafel see a very idyllic life, lifestyle and setting. For the most part, this is true. What fascinates me and what I witnessed first hand today, is the glorious complexity of humans co-existing. In mainstream battery hen living, I for one, had a minuscule input into the running of the community and settlement I was residing in. Here, people are having to organise and discuss all the same issues councils do. And a whole lot more.

Of course, here you also have those that attend most if not all meetings, as well as others who only do so when issues directly affect or pertain to them.

The Diary And Path Of The Warless Warrior

I feel in this environment and structure, it is far easier to have your say and make a difference. That said, the daunting myriad of rules, issues and protocol could seriously make one NOT wish to reside in a community of ANY description. In my opinion the benefits far outweigh this and I empathise with those in this community who wish to place trust in others to wade through the quagmire on their behalf.

An important proposal was raised and agreed to, which was the fostering by Lammas of another low impact settlement using the template of Tir Y Gafel.

There is a feeling inside me akin to being present at the birth of Christ and bearing witness to the beginning of an extremely important movement. I am also the bearer of a terrible sadness when I realise money currently prevents my entry into this incredible life. As our stay continues, I foresee expansion and the opportunities that brings, melting away as those with the cash leap frog their way in front of us. The pain of this would be crushing and the fear of this alone could be enough to make me want to leave, just to avoid that possibility.

I will not be ruled by fear. With that in mind I feel if we can spend some more time here, providence will provide a doorway.

Woe betide the man who disturbs the pregnant
beast.

Friday 12/11/10

Yesterday was windy to say the least. The prevailing wind in these conditions is troublesome, but would not appear to be as damaging nor as mischievous as turbulent gusts. Their ferocity prompted me to baton down the hatches and place straw bales at the base of the awning. This action was reinforced by the placement of chunks of concrete salvaged from a shattered slab, placed along the awning skirt.

Nature called around 17:00 and it was then I noticed the compost toilet had been damaged. The tent material used to cover the windward side had been shredded rendering the inside completely exposed. But when ya gotta go, ya gotta go. Even if the door decides to twat you across the shins, then disappear, providing all with a view of your activity. A most excellent form of laxative.

After a very cold and hurried dump, I repaired it by screwing a cladding of slabwood in place.

Am finding myself increasingly enjoying the time spent cutting kindling for the fire. What with the realisation I have another child in the making, its good to find somewhere to be alone. Its hardly a huge surprise, nor accident, but remains a shock to the system. A shift in how I perceive the future. A change in needs and priorities.

Now the two man tent containing logs and brewing kit is my sanctuary. Would prefer the barrels to be full of beer. Well one has hawthorn brew in. Not enough for my liking however.

Found out yesterday that two weeks ago, my best friends long term girlfriend dumped him seemingly for no reason. He'd been in a mess and rang to ask if he could stay for a week, see me, volunteer and generally get a change of scenery.

Emma agreed to this, and he booked a week off work. Then she changed her mind.

If Moses can't come to the mountain, the mountain must come to Moses. Figure that this will be mutually beneficial. I need space, and he needs me. My face can be his change of scenery. Emma might kick off but she has no right to decide who can or can't visit Lammas.

Saturday 13/11/10

All around are the visible signs autumn is here and winter is approaching.

The recent high winds have dislodged the leaves that have died, and the trees now look skeletal and bare.

All this death will pave the way for rebirth. But death has come calling too close for comfort this year, seeing fit to end the life of a good friend of mine. At present, I know scant few details, but a man not living past his 24th winter is a sobering thought indeed. His loss has weighed heavy on my mind, occupying thoughts and clouding others.

If nothing else, I am reminded that whatever my reservations about having another baby are, he never got the chance to father one.

To my friend Keith Jefferies, who died 11/11/10

The message I wrote on his Facebook wall when I found out:

"I find this page extremely hard reading. It goes from friendly banter and chat concerning day to day life. Then posts of "get well soon". To Commiserations and Eulogies.

There's an anger inside me I can't direct.
There's a feeling of betrayal by the forces upon which I trusted and depend.
An anguish that an individual such as he, has gone where I cannot yet go.
Above all, there is a gut wrenching guilt. The guilt we all dread which cannot be assuaged by apology. But its an apology I will

make anyway.

Keith. I am sorry I didn't give you more of my time. You gave me yours, and for that I will thank you eternally. Please forgive me.

My time will come, as yours has done. You have led and I shall follow. Knowing this I shall not fear death. Because I know you're waiting for me.

Til then Keith, I will miss you, and mourn your passing. We all will."

To his brother Mark, this message;

"My good friend Keith...

I went to school with Keith, a valued and trusted friend. I'm deeply shocked and saddened.

As a brothers love is so great as to be valued and cherished, his loss is all the more terrible and the grief that much more severe.

I am so sorry. A lot of people are thinking of you, in that take some comfort.

Whoever God is, may He bless you, and all your family."

Wednesday 17/11/10

Levelling Kits foundations 14/11/10

Slaked lime to be used in the mortar 14/11/10

Kits Lime Pit 14/11/10

The Diary And Path Of The Warless Warrior

Slightly squeeze a ketchup bottle then open it. I dare ya.

Am so tired, I nearly put off writing this entry. Am only doing so due to my horrendous short term memory.

Earlier this week I found two adverts for static caravans. One was a really cheap and shabby one on eBay. The auction was at £75 so I over generously put what I thought was a losing bid of £400. Problem was I won the damn thing. This of course happened before I was told it would cost £750 to transport! Being the auction had a couple of days to run, I continued looking and found one in Pencader, outside Carmarthen for £600. The photos were fantastic... The caravan wasn't. Neglected for five years, the gas safety certificate said it all. Next inspection due '07. Great.

Still, I rang down the list of transport companies the man had given me. £350, £300 plus vat etc etc. Being 12ft wide meant it required an escort, thereby bumping up the price considerably.

The Diary And Path Of The Warless Warrior

Thoroughly dejected we returned home. It was then that I received a belated reply from one of the companies. After a bit of chit chat, it transpired they were based a couple of miles away and had a static available. They wanted £1100 but with a bit of bargaining and mostly kindheartedness on his part, he agreed to not only sell but deliver it for £900! I said we'd take a look...

That night we went to bed very much encouraged. Unfortunately, it wasn't just our spirits that were high that night. After buffeting us steadily, at 05:00 the wind finally ripped up the awning and flung it over the caravan in an almighty cacophony of bending steel, tearing fabric, catapulted belongings, falling tables and finally a thump of sodden canvas slapped over the roof of the caravan.

Shit.

My first thought was... f**k it. I'll deal with it in the morning. Until I realised canvas was smothering the chimney of our freshly stoked fire. Bollocks.

So out in to the roaring abyss I went to sort out one god awful mess and salvage whatever could be saved. Just doing the minimum took an hour with Ayres' help.

The Diary And Path Of The Warless Warrior

The Morning After.

The Diary And Path Of The Warless Warrior

The Battered Cowling.

Like the Titanic, I too could've avoided disaster...

Neither Al Qeada nor Hitler was responsible. Hard to believe I
know.

Not the view I paid for...
Still, it sparked a limerick.

The Diary And Path Of The Warless Warrior

There once was a caravan in Wales,
That was subject to terrible gales,
They woke up one morning, minus an Awning,
With only an outline of Bales...

The most part of today was spent mopping up, and eventually re-erecting a rather poorly awning.

The Diary And Path Of The Warless Warrior

You've heard of that caravan in Wales,
That was subject to terrible gales,
Well the awnings back on,
The wind and rain have now gone,
And silenced the groans and the wails.

Job done I went to start the car ready for viewing the static. But
there was more... prompting this message to Emma.

We own a small caravan in Wales,
About which people have heard many tales,
Please don't think me mean, or cause a scene,
But I've just found a crack in our windscreen.

I suspect a leak around the glass allowed water to freeze
resulting in a vehicular form of frost heave.

Finally, we viewed this static.

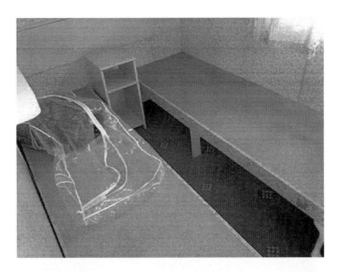

The Diary And Path Of The Warless Warrior

Was in a small mess inside having just been transported. The big plus with this is it was in service on a holiday park until this summer. The only downside was a missing vent cap lost in transit had allowed water in the kitchen. Tomorrow the vendor is coming to approve our proposed transport route with the driver, before we commit to anything. If it gets the go ahead I'll be bloody relieved.

Relayed our woes to friends and family and received this reply from our old neighbour.

There once was a couple from Stroud,
Who decided to break from the crowd.
Although their new life,
was full of trouble and strife,
Of themselves they were very proud.

The Diary And Path Of The Warless Warrior

Although it contains an 'inside' joke, I couldn't resist a retort.

There once was an actor next door,
Whose performances left us in awe.
We do miss him so,
but we just had to go.
And hope he wears clothes a bit more.

So life is currently a rollercoaster of highs and lows right now.
My day turned to night as I screwed the awning skirting into
some logs reinforced with batons to prevent it shredding itself.
knowing our luck right now, it will only serve to form a deadly
volley of missiles smashing through our roof the next time God
farts.

Aww well, one more limerick then bed.

For Nigel, my number one fan, who believes I should be
crowned Lammas poet laureate.
We live just outside the Presellis,
To Narbeth we take all our smellies.
The wind is a pain, so is the rain,
If you come, you'd better bring wellies.

The Diary And Path Of The Warless Warrior

Monday 22/11/10

Having trouble casting my mind back to know where to begin.
Have been upto so much, last Thursday seems a lifetime ago,
but I'll do my best.
Football - Thursday was the debut of a second team in the
league, created due to the fact we had so many guys wanting to
play. The first teams fixture was before us, and they put in an
honourable performance losing 8-3. The second team, for
which I played, faced the league champions of 6 consecutive
years. We got slaughtered. A glorious massacre at 17-2. The
consolation for me, was that I scored the first of our goals. That
game was on another level, and left me forced to re-evaluate
my fitness level. Will be sticking to Mondays until my stamina
and aerobic fitness is on par.

Friday and Saturday I went with Ayres and Kit to pick up two
trailer loads of very very well rotted manure. So well rotted
that my first step in the pile saw my welly disappear and my
leg saturated in poo juice. Nice.
Saturday afternoon, I sat in on a talk by a local fruit tree expert
who really knew his stuff. His orchard has over 1000 species
with no two trees the same. He is bringing back lost native
British varieties by importing graftwood from Tasmania and
other parts of the empire as was.
17:00 Kit and I set off for Kilgetty to pick up some ash whips
and saplings following an advert I'd seen on Freecycle. After a
long chat with the chap we were invited back in the day where,
within reason, we could take what we liked from his woodland.
A very valuable contact!
Despite having already had a long and productive day, Ayres

told Kit and I to dress warm and dry and report at 20:30 for a 'mission'.

We ended up hiking over the Presellis until gone 02:00. The night was clear and the moon full, making for a fantastic experience.

Sunday, yesterday, Emma Kit and I planted ash and in the evening had a brilliant homemade curry.

Boy did I sleep well!

Woke up this morning thinking of catching up on the blog, however my morning cigarette was interrupted by a delivery of 20 tons of stone. Heigh Ho Heigh Ho, its off to work I go...

The Diary And Path Of The Warless Warrior

The Diary And Path Of The Warless Warrior

Very well rotted indeed.

A group photograph taken a while back. The photographer
kindly sent each of us a copy.

I missed this shot. You can tell its lacking

something :-)

The Diary And Path Of The Warless Warrior

Planting the ash whips. Should be ready to harvest in 5-10 years.

Wednesday 24/11/10

Once again, there is trouble in paradise. 10:00 Tuesday morning began another Lammas Committee meeting. All very routine until the last agenda item. "Long term volunteers : financial/legal/privacy and how do we get rid of those who do not want to leave?"

A valid agenda item as it is written. Pertaining to another volunteer who wouldn't cook for themselves (privacy issue for the leaseholder) was of foreign nationality (legal?) broke (financial) and now didn't want to leave. Unfortunately, thanks to someone who I shall kindly allow to remain anonymous, it morphed into a debate when said person randomly brought up that Kit intended to allow us to inhabit a static on his plot. In my opinion this was most regrettable. Obviously Ms Anonymous had motives...

First off, yet again, there were wild inaccuracies, very few facts and subsequently fearful speculation. The same recipe for disaster that occurred not a month prior.

Secondly, this arrangement does not exist yet. Far better would be to find out exactly what is being proposed, gain clarity and move forward. Most interesting was the fact that despite Ms Anonymous knowing the facts, us having confided in her on this matter, she failed to elaborate to the group. Preferring to slink back and allow the mess to erupt.

It was proposed that all volunteers sign a contract with an end date. A residents meeting was suggested in order to discuss the matter and ascertain what exactly should go on the next committee meeting agenda. Despite us being one of the areas of focus of this residents meeting, we were not invited to attend and provide our side of the matter.

The residents meeting, I believe to be a sensible thing. But we couldn't help coming away feeling stabbed in the back, unvalued and unappreciated. Just disposable items ready to be replaced.

That is probably due to not being in a position with any form of power. Therefore our reaction was to reach for that which is in our power. The ability to stay, or rather, leave.

As the dust has settled, so have emotions, but an uneasy air hangs like a mist in the valley. The committee asked that things be put on hold for two weeks. What they don't know is that we have already postponed the caravans delivery three times. Following the verdict, we delayed twice more and now the vendor is understandably wanting to know what to do. With this in mind we've agreed to delivery next Monday. This has already prompted the question from Ms Anonymous "Why have you not waited, at least until after the residents meeting?" This is unfair and unjustified in my opinion for the following reasons.

It is wrong for people to assume we have any power. Let alone, the power to engage in any activity that does not carry the consent of a plotholder.

It is unfair, in light of the many previous occasions we have already postponed and waited.

The other factor to consider is that we are not out to be defiant, undermine, or upset people. We have simply been presented with a wonderful and generous opportunity to better our current situation, our hearts and intentions are pure. I have faith that all considered, people will see truth and reason, and see us for the valuable asset we are. Kit seems to...

Sunday 28/11/10

The nights are long, and the days are hard. This is winter, Olde English, or should I say, Olde Welsh style.

Last night was cold, temperatures dipping below -4C. Over ground pipes frozen. Roof vents sealed by the elements. If you're not checking your heat source through the night, you will invariably wake up to a frost bitten duvet at the very least. Our wood consumption has rocketed to two overflowing buckets a day. This is opposed to one lasting two days. Our stockpile is diminished and in urgent need of replenishment. Thursday the 25th saw our first flake of snow, with more forecast.

I've managed to contract a cold and a cough. This has meant me being relegated to light duties for fear of triggering bouts of rib crunching, ear popping, coughing fits. Throw in a strained back muscle, and existence gets miserable.

This modicum of discomfort has gone a little way to illustrating how challenging winter was to our ancestors. I recall reading books containing the phrase "might not survive the winter". Experiencing what I am, perhaps those words were not the melodramatic exaggeration I once thought them to be. Is it any wonder why, only in the last 100-200 years, the life expectancy of the average man has surpassed the age of 40? One of the reasons that, at present, I might reach 60 can be partly attributed to the fact I can pay some bloke £40 and VOILA, another few months of processed firewood appears...

In other news. Our little family has acquired a 6 week old feline addition aptly named Eira, welsh for snow. (Despite being a grey slush colour) This choice of label stems from the snowy, bollock chilling day we picked her up. Unsurprisingly her and I can now be found practically hugging the wood burner.

Took Fran to an adventure park called Folly Farm near Narbeth. She had a great time and I got a hot meal that contained a lot of meat. Need I say more.

The Log Store - If I were to store logs in there again, I'd put them on a pallet.

The Diary And Path Of The Warless Warrior

The Diary And Path Of The Warless Warrior

Camera Boredom

The Diary And Path Of The Warless Warrior

The Tasmanian Devil

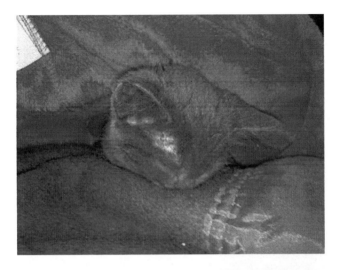

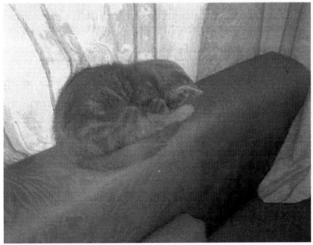

The Diary And Path Of The Warless Warrior

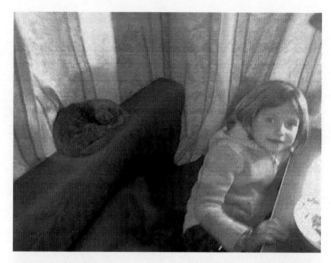

The Diary And Path Of The Warless Warrior

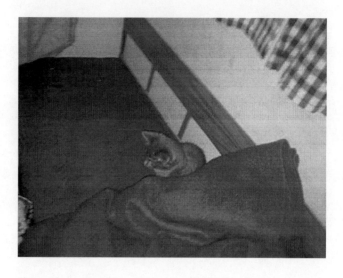

Monday 29/11/10

Frances' 7th Birthday. She has been counting down for days and here it is. Today also happens to be the delivery day for our static caravan. As if the route wasn't narrow and challenging enough, there is a lot of ice on the roads that seems perfectly impervious to the efforts of the sun. The driver did a fantastic job and was therefore horribly crestfallen to see I had ticked the 'damaged in transit' box. I had noticed a vent was ripped open, something I am certain I would have noted prior to purchasing, very minor, but no amount of downplaying could restore the mans hurt pride.

The rest of the day was spent manoeuvring and prat arsing about, but by 15:00 we were done. During this time Fran played with her presents, something I never felt I was allowed to do for long enough as a kid.

17:00 we went swimming, something Fran has wanted to do since she finished going to school. This was perfect as it meant showers all round. A pleasure normally, but a luxury and a treat now all the pipes on site are frozen!

The treats didn't end there as we finished the day with fish and chips. Upon our return home, we were all very ready for bed.

A Violin. From A Relative, I Don't Have £400
Odd...

The Damage

The Diary And Path Of The Warless Warrior

Simple Things Please Simple Minds...

Thursday 02/12/10

Have been umming and ahhing about the best thing to do with regards to getting a wood burner in the static.
Our resources are severely limited, so limited we were nearly forced to take out the burner we have in this little caravan. That wouldn't really have worked either however, as its only 2.5kw and would be heating a poorly insulated space.
Finally I was forced to make the call to my folks to beg for emergency bail out money. This is something I honestly loath doing. God bless them, they came through and we have a burner and flue system ordered and hopefully arriving within the next 24 hours.

Ran out of wood last night. Thankfully another load came just in time. The previous lot lasted 3 months in a 2.5kw burner. It's therefore safe to assume this load will only last 1.5 months... Still £35 isn't bad compared to the heating bill of a house.

As a measure of how much wood we're burning and kindling I'm having to cut, my trusty old car boot axe broke :-(
Have kept the head and intend on repairing, however, in the meantime I've bought a Fiskars axe with a lifetime guarantee. That should last!

The Diary And Path Of The Warless Warrior

We've nearly run out of paraffin. So I've switched the battery over to the caravans 12 volt circuit. Am pretty upset I didn't do it sooner really. the lights are brilliant with the juiciest being just 15 watts! The two we use mainly I think are 5 watts each. So 10w/12 volts = 0.8333*amps. Our battery is 110 amp hour so at 80% efficiency 88 amp hours. 88ah/0.8333* = 105.6 hours of light! That has got to be cheaper than paraffin!

Tuesday 07/12/10

Jesus Christ! I literally have not stopped since Thursday. I have done so much, I can't clearly distinguish the days apart, much less relate events back in much detail. The best I can do is summarise what I do remember. Friday morning, I read a copy of the draft agenda for today's meeting. Was upset and dismayed to read two letters in it written by the business manager. These letters, in my opinion, were full of inaccuracies, misinformation and parts of a conversation I'd had with him taken out of context and misquoted. Discussing this swallowed up the entire morning, and before I knew it, it was time to take Ayres to the station for his foray to London. Upon my return, Emma, myself and Kit made a resupply run to Crymych. When we were done, the day was gone.

Saturday - an extremely busy day. The temperatures rarely got above freezing which meant the nights rain had frozen turning the track way into an ice rink. It also made the ground look wet and muddy, yet completely solid. Really weird.
Being the 4th it was Emma's birthday. As my present to her, I moved our touring caravan up to its new spot beside the static, and did the bulk of everything else. Her birthday means all of our little family have now celebrated a birthday here.

Sunday - Clean up operation. After pissing about with electrics. Saturday night I rigged up a battery from the car in order for Fran to watch a movie. Unfortunately, because it was raining, I moved the inverter into the dry underneath the static caravan in the dark and inadvertently touched the casing against the positive terminal. POP! Lights out.

The Diary And Path Of The Warless Warrior

Kit was kind enough to cut some slabs that will be used as thermal mass and protection around the wood burner. After all that I spent an hour or so ensuring Ayres and Marianne's land was left exactly how we found it. Unfortunately my electrical nightmare was set to continue.

Just before the sun fully set, I managed to rig up the solar panels and create a far safer and more satisfactory electrical set up. Sadly the inverter we'd borrowed decided to pack in and display a fault light, as well as my charge regulator no longer displaying voltage and seemingly also go on strike. BOLLOCKS!

Monday - Road trip. Once again, it was off to Llanelli to replace the inverter and charge regulator for the second time. £20 of fuel gone. As Emma said, this life is supposed to be simpler and less reliant on money, but we can't afford it!

That said, I and most others can't afford conventional life. She's right, but wrong. Wrong, because the things we cannot afford such as diesel, insurance, mobile phone bill, and electrics are non essential for survival.

Luckily we got the items replaced without any problems and in fact came out better off. The next inverter up was on offer and cheaper than ours. So we were told we could swap for that and take other stuff to make up the difference. We were at a loss as to what else we needed. I wanted a remote control helicopter, but settled on a battery charger for Kit...

Emma needed to buy a bra, so she and Fran went touring the naughty sections of various shops whilst Kit and I checked out

boots and clothes in T.K.Maxx.
The car died on the journey there most likely due to the cold
and bio-diesel, so we put in some mineral diesel, but this made
us late for Ayres who needed picking up after returning from
his trip to London. Felt bad about that...

Tuesday - Meeting. These meetings are obviously a black hole
for productive time. Another 5 hour sitting.
This particular gathering was farcical. I couldn't help but draw
analogies from George Orwell's 'Animal Farm' and '1984'. It is
quite apparent that here at Lammas there is a power struggle
now the Farmer has been evicted, and its definitely the pigs
who think they run the show.
The 1984 side came from letters written by the business
manager, or should I say the 'Ministry of Truth'. These were
written after I talked to him, a discussion in which I wanted to
be absolutely clear and frank, especially when the matter was
agenda'd for this meeting. So imagine my horror and disgust
when these words were twisted and taken out of context in
order to support his delusions. His letters read like WWII
propaganda pamphlets. The inaccuracies so wild, it could have
been interpreted as a joke. The irony is it also came to his
attention that someone had written a damning article about
Lammas in a local publication, and his response condemned it
as "...falsehoods presented as fact". Well, Well! Its easy to spot
when someone is pulling the same tricks you are!

The meeting started with the usual crap and it was obvious
everyone wanted to get to the issue at hand, unfortunately,
when it did, the meeting broke down into what can only be

described as a slanging match. The sort of pathetic behaviour you witness on a primary school playground, etiquette was forgotten. At the one point I spoke, and tried to clarify the truth as opposed to the published nonsense, I was interrupted by Ms Anonymous, who was either lying, distracted by her child or just not paying attention. This completely threw me off and I watched as the meeting degenerated. A business/committee meeting. My God. Lord Sugar would have been speechless. Gross professional misconduct is being kind.

At the previous meeting, those present were informed Lammas had been represented at the Welsh Assembly and the message was "The world is watching". That's worrying! I don't think anyone here would want the world watching right now! Lammas would definitely not be praised and lauded in the future.

One resident related his past experience in a "dysfunctional housing co-op". It is quite apparent to me that "Sorry mate, you're in one!"

Sickened, saddened and disillusioned is how I and others are feeling. Lammas is described as trying to emulate a traditional English village... well its not the idyllic one they were aiming for. Its one infected by all the crap that people bring, set in a beautiful part of the Welsh countryside.

Fear and Loathing in Lammas

Wednesday 08/12/10

Our cold, very large cool box has now been transformed into a comfortable abode. The wood burner is in!

Our 6.5kw JA014 Wood Burning Stove

This installation was a far cry from the last time when all I had was a pair of tin snips and a stanley knife. This time we had cordless drills, cordless jigsaws, set squares, crayons, self tapping screws, the lot. All thanks to Kit with the kit. Kits Kit. So this evening, it was absolutely brilliant to sit down with Kit and share a home made lamb korma by a roaring fire.
It was -6C that night and I was up at 04:00 getting the bad boy going again. Anyway. Thanks Mum and Dad for the £500! Has made us warm that's for sure.

Thursday 09/12/10

The bitter taste of Tuesdays so called Committee Meeting has started to subside. There are still rumblings and grumblings amongst the residents, and I forecast further tremours and aftershocks following the next meeting, scheduled for this Tuesday.

Kit and I occupied our bodies and minds doing what little we can on a frozen but defrosting building pad. The lime sitting in two trugs is still frozen solid and unusable. This made brick laying impossible, so we had to satisfy ourselves by marking out the edges with fluorescent string and metal line pins. Even these put up a fight...

Am mindful the blog is being neglected as it is simply too uncomfortable to update whilst sitting in a freezing agricultural barn. So this evening I have been trying to do it in the luxurious warmth of the static caravan. Its taking a while....

Friday 10/12/10

Temperatures have risen and the ground is thawing. Now our carefully measured lines on the building pad that were taut, are now slack and adrift.

Aside from odd jobs, the only thing to do is take Kit to the train station. He'll be away until Wednesday. Will miss him but I have plenty to keep me occupied.

1) Lay a pathway to the static. The thawed ground is now soaked and muddy.

2) Turn over the vegetable beds ready for planting around January.

3) Dig a 100m trench 6 inches deep in order to fence an

enclosure for our rabbit farming venture.

Not a long list, but a tidy amount to do. Will get cracking tomorrow.

Saturday 11/12/10

Got item 1 done. Began by trying to sift and wash the stone from the mounds of soil currently deposited in the walled garden. But this was too slow and time consuming. Instead I smashed up some large lumps of slate used to make the track way. This too, was time consuming but was a damn sight quicker than washing off sodden, clay rich mud.
14:30 Emma had an hour appointment with the mid wife. After this we headed to Cardigan for fuel and sweeties, as well as a resupply in Tesco. Am very much looking forward to the day when this is no longer a necessity.

Sunday 12/12/10

Sunshine! Better wash the solar panels! Our mobiles have been suffering due to the past overcast days and the fact the car inverter doesn't seem to be doing the job.
Got one job done during my morning cigarette. The rear door of the static is scraping the frame. Probably due to the axle not yet being bricked up and supported. Can't raise it as my car bottle jack can't cope. The answer? Deflate the tire. Door fixed. Caravan level. Job done.
The rest of the day was spent preparing the vegetable beds.

Emma came out to help for a bit before lunch and again as the light was fading. Have managed to get 4 of 8 dug, and one strip spread 3/4 of the way with muck. That 3/4 was a whole trailer load which shocked me.
Was aching and very tired but managed to spend three hours desperately trying to catch up on the blog. Same again tomorrow methinks.

The Diary And Path Of The Warless Warrior

Monday 13/12/10

The chocolate advent calendar may not contain the highest grade of confectionery but it is serving the purpose of reminding me Christmas is rapidly approaching. I honestly believe, without it, and if no-one reminded me, I'd completely forget. And have the most wonderful Christmas ever. Would be cheaper too.

More preparation of veggie beds, one of which was nearly completely reclaimed and was a real pig. Despite the burning back muscles and physical exertion I couldn't be happier. Many would find that disconcerting. I must be a very old 25 years of age. Still, gardening may be regarded as a pastime reserved for older, retired English gents, but I tell you what, I'll be bloody chuffed if I'm still capable of doing what I've just done in 40-50 years time!

Here's to all those misunderstood and deceptively fit, retired backyard gardeners out there!

Row 4 Done

Row 5

Row 6

The Diary And Path Of The Warless Warrior

Row 7

Row 8. Admired by Gwyn.

Tuesday 14/12/10

Spoke to Kit this morning, following a missed call from him
last night. After it emerged it was of no great importance, I
proudly informed him all the vegetable beds were now done.
To which he replied words to the effect of "Thank you, that's
excellent, hope the fruit bushes and globe artichokes are ok".
SHIT! The bushes were fine, they were obvious, but what the
hell do globe artichokes look like? I asked vaguely which ones
the were assuring him that all was well, but couldn't press him
without letting on that I'd most likely flipped them over and
chopped them into the ground with a spade...
A hurried root (no pun intended) and rummage in the pile of
grass and dead stuff revealed 9-12 healthy look specimens that
I'd kept to one side in case of just such an occurrence. These
were re-planted swiftly and <u>very</u> neatly in as close to their
original place as possible. Phew. Another meeting to attend, not
quite as upsetting as last week.

Came back to find Justin had returned from a long weekend
away. Had a coffee. Faffed about with the fire. Time passed.
Just before sundown I went to get water, just so happened
Justin was about to do the same. Explained to him that Kit was
due back tomorrow, and told him about my near cock up with
the artichokes.
Justin graciously informed me that what I had replanted were
sprout plants. <u>Not</u> artichokes. Oh crap.
Another rummage and fretful excavation produced 4 or 5 very
upset, very dirty artichokes. No matter how much I caress them
or fiddle with them, they are determined to betray me. They
remain looking like someone dug them up, flipped them over

and buried them.
I hope Kit isn't too upset...

Fire TV. Consistently better than the crap on Freeview. Even
appeals to a feline audience.

The Diary And Path Of The Warless Warrior

The Diary And Path Of The Warless Warrior

These, are globe artichokes.

The Diary And Path Of The Warless Warrior

These, are not.

Wednesday 15/12/10

An early-ish start being that Emma had an appointment with the midwife. An appointment she had in fact lost sleep over and was abjectly dreading. They wanted her blood. Four vials of it. My presence was required, about this there obviously could be no argument. Frances would be left in the company of strangers and charged with amusing herself. Such was Emma's fear, she was quite at ease with this neglect.

To distract Emma, and also deter my own boredom, I regaled the midwife with my artichoke fiasco. It would appear people find my horticultural ignorance frightfully amusing. Or just frightful.

Back home I raked the beds until Beth, another volunteer, dropped by to say farewell and give Justin a lift on his Christmas visit home. She won't be returning choosing instead to head to mid-Wales come the New Year in her converted post van.

A few hours later Kit arrived back, with his step father John and some miscellaneous items and luxuries. Some of these luxuries were devoured that evening in a spaghetti carbanara we shared.

On and off I've been reading ***The Complete Book of Self Sufficiency*** by John Seymour.. In his introduction, it is clear we share the same views. He says "...Man was not *meant* to be a one job animal. We do not thrive as parts of a machine. We are intended by nature to be diverse, to do diverse things, to have many skills." I couldn't agree more with the words "Self sufficiency does not mean 'going back' to the acceptance of a lower standard of living. On the contrary, it is striving for a higher standard of living, for food which is fresh and organically grown and good, for the good life in pleasant surroundings, for the health of body and peace of mind which come with hard varied work in the open air, and for the satisfaction that comes from doing difficult and intricate jobs well and successfully". With this in mind, I recall an article I read in The Guardian newspaper only a day or two before, in which it stated that a household that earns less than £16000 per annum is considered in this country to be poor.

We are not earning anywhere near £16000. I personally never have done. But never before have I considered myself poor. I have never gone hungry. Never have I or my little family been cold and powerless to remedy it.

This remains to be true, and yet now we earn nothing, subsidised as we are to the tune of £90 odd a week. By the standards set by others, we are currently amongst the poorest people in the country today. Yes, this entry is being written by paraffin lantern, but that is because I'd like to save our solar energy for another time/appliance.

To the outsider this could be seen as a mark of our poverty. But the real truth is we've never had it so good. We generally buy local organic meat and vegetables, (lamb that's grazed on the wild windswept sides of the Presellis should be organic...) we sleep until we wish to rise. I work until I am tired/bored, whichever comes sooner. I certainly never work if I don't feel upto it.

Admittedly the latter is rare as to date I haven't suffered an illness or accident that has rendered me incapable.

We live in a beautiful valley near the sea, in a part of Wales people pay to visit and often travel great distances to do so. Poor in money, rich in life. I couldn't be happier.

The Diary And Path Of The Warless Warrior

If I may I would like to quote John Seymour once more, this time from the foreword of his brilliant book.
"There are very few processes in this book that I have not performed myself; albeit, perhaps, some of them ineptly. Does this make me a jack-of-all-trades and master of none? Well I'd rather be that than a person who can only do one thing. To me that would be Hell. I have embarked on many an enterprise without the faintest idea of how to do it - but I have always ended up with the thing done and with a great deal more knowledge than when I started". That quote is both a view I share, and an accurate description of my current lifestyle. Tomorrow, brick laying!

Thursday 16/12/10

The North wind has returned, bringing rain and snow. Not the best conditions in which to start laying bricks and mixing lime mortar...

Despite the mix coming out far too wet and sloppy, we have nonetheless laid four corners of the building and shall leave them to dry and observe what happens. More snow forecast for Friday and Saturday and some cold nights. Luckily, with this night forecast as being the coldest, Frances has by chance been invited to sleep over at Simon and Jasmines. A very lucky little girl, on one count for being able to stay in a beautiful hand built house, and another for being warm and able to sleep well in that house as opposed to our static caravan.

My lantern is now running low on paraffin, so I shall sign off and turn in.

Good Night.

The Diary And Path Of The Warless Warrior

The Diary And Path Of The Warless Warrior

Friday 17/12/10

Paul and Hoppi invited everyone to theirs for a house warming now their live in barn is completed and habitable. They have both done a fantastic job and are justified in their pride. Of course the opportunity to hang a door with Nigel and Cassie and engage in yet more carpentry was understandably something Paul wished to pass on.

Laid out on the table were various sweet treats including stollen and home made chocolate nests, accompanied by mulled wine. Very nice indeed.

What was also nice, was to be able to meet and socialise with the community outside of an official meeting.

We went on to Simon and Jasmines to eat a pork casserole we'd cooked earlier that day. Once that hit my stomach, I was ready for bed!

The Diary And Path Of The Warless Warrior

The Finished Article

Saturday 18/12/10

Nigel from next door popped round during a morning game of chess with Kit. Primarily, he wanted to 'Jones' some tobacco. He also wished to know if we were planning on venturing to Crymych that day. No one else is able it would seem due to the snow and ice. My mighty 4x4 cares not a jot for it. Not only did I end up with a shopping list , but also a shovel and a tow rope. Unfortunately, without grit or perhaps snow chains, my truck couldn't grip enough to tow. We managed to extricate one car after the neighbours son freed his van, but that was it. Good deeds done for the day, and neighbours resupplied, the evening soon skipped past as Kit and I played a few more games of chess.
3 more centimetres of snow fell and the night got extremely cold. I dare say my 4x4 will be called upon again.

Sunday 19/12/10

More vehicle recovery and rescue, as well as another resupply run. Took Kit, Jasmine and Ted into Crymych with Jasmine adamant this was the 'Last Trip' as the world would end in the coming days...she paid me a fiver for fuel which was kind. After this I gave Nigel a lift to his car, followed him until he was safely parked at the bottom of the trackway with the other vehicles and gave him a ride a home.

Vehicle Advert?

Panels Down To 0% Efficiency. Ice On The Inside Of The
Windows.

The Diary And Path Of The Warless Warrior

The Diary And Path Of The Warless Warrior

Carols at Cassies

The Diary And Path Of The Warless Warrior

Monday 20/12/10

Nigels wife Cassie had asked if we could take her to Clunderwyn station as she was volunteering in a shop in Carmarthen, this tied in nicely as we were already driving to Narbeth to take Kits cat, or Kits Kat, to be spayed. As it happened, we then drove to Carmarthen as it made alot of sense due to the size of the place and that way we could save Cassie a train journey.

Had a good time mooching, and eating fresh pasties from a Taste of Cornwall shop.

Met up with Cassie. She wondered whether we could pick up Nigels Solstice present - a red leather chair from Narbeth, went well with the "Bah Humbug" hat I bought him. This was fine as we'd need to go back there for the cat. It fitted in the boot, and Nigel got his gift in time.

Had just settled in front of the wood burner with a welcome cup of coffee when the phone rang. A delivery van was stuck at the bottom of the trackway, teetering over a ditch. Would I answer the call? Cors ah wud!

Another rescue under the belt, and it was nearing 18:00. Now I had said I'd pass on football, but the idea of a shower in a warm environment twisted my arm...

Emma wasn't happy, she and Fran had found me a copy of The Muppet Christmas Carol. on DVD and were looking forward to watching it together. Managed to squeeze it in before footy, but it was touch and go as our battery was very low. A combination of a small dvd player and a 12v transformer of Kits was much more efficient than the inverter.

Upon my return around 23:00 I was glad to get into bed, but this wasn't to be, the grate had been left open and the fire burnt out. The caravan was freezing and we were out of kindling. 02:00, the fire was up to temperature, and I stiffly climbed into bed...

Gwyn sensing somethings up...

Tuesday 21/12/10

A chance to mong out at Nigel and Cassies roundhouse whilst the womenfolk crafted various items. Green man thingymabobs and felt stuff.

Around 15:00, I couldn't put off the trip to Bwlchygroes for gas any longer. Supplied with a shopping list for others, we stopped off in Crymych. Whilst sitting in the car waiting for Emma, I received a call from Jane wondering if we were out and about. Her son Jake was due back from school at 16:00, and her car was parked a 50 minute walk away so could we pick him up? Only meant a 20 minute wait for us. In that time I called ahead to warn Nick the Gas of our intentions. His words were, "careful as you go, don't touch the brakes or clutch, its bloody lethal. Put her in low and let her go". Thanks Nick. As it happened all went well and another day ended safely.

Wednesday 22/12/10

A day of departures. A night of disturbances. Emma has a cough. Trouble is, she likes to snuggle into me during the night for warmth. This meant me suffering being kneed in the back for most of the night, then when I could take it no more and eventually turned over, I got coughed at in the face.

As I wasn't sleeping, I got up at 04:00 in the belief lying there was wasting valuable packing time.

06:00 Car was loaded, warmed up and all ready to go. Dropped Kit off at Clunderwyn station at 06:30, no problem. Then our luck turned. For a while now the electrics and batteries haven't been right, with the heater noticeably draining charge. As long as it wasn't on for too long, we were normally ok.

Now we were in trouble. There was no charge going to the batteries and they were nearly dead. What was also worrying was if I sped up, the voltage *decreased*. It wasn't long before I was forced to stop. The dashboard was dim, the lights draining more charge, the windscreen blurred with ice inside and out. Things were looking grim. By stopping to allow what little charge there was to get to the batteries and clearing the windscreen, we made nervous progress, but were running out of fuel.

This was getting even more grim. I knew we'd be better off if we could make it to Carmarthen Tescos to fuel up. We'd also be better off again once the sun rose. We'd no longer need the heater or the lights. With this in mind, I risked the last few dual carriageway miles on sidelights and half gave a sigh of relief when we limped into the filling station. Half, because I was pretty sure the car wouldn't start if I followed the rules and turned the engine off. I was right. The two new batteries were as dead as two large and expensive electrical Dodos.

A really nice chap in a red Daihatsu 4x4 jump started us and we were back on our way, despite the indicators nearly killing the engine whenever we turned off.

At Cardiff services I made some calls. One to Lawrence, our mechanic, another to my Dad. Lawrence told me a new alternator would be £300-£400. My Dad advised we turn back home.

Emma was having none of it, so onwards we ploughed.

Arrived at Emma's mums just gone 11:30. After unloading, I took the truck to the garage and walked home. On my way, I bumped into Dianne, Em's Mum. She gave me a lift back as she was going home herself.

She parked her car on the main drag as she couldn't get into their road.

This prompted me to start shovelling snow off the road at 14:14.

Made good progress with a couple of passers by expressing their gratitude. Wasn't really a selfless act. Felt it was rather sensible.

The council weren't going to clear it. I could have been British and just grumbled. But if clearing the road myself meant Dianne would have to park on the main road and add to the congestion, all the better. It did cross my mind I could be cheeky enough to bill the council for my time hehe.

Whilst I was out clearing, a Fed-ex van got stuck just beyond where I'd got to. A colleague of his turned up and two hours later he was on his way. Again, I tried my luck. When the chap thanked me I told him if Fed-Ex felt generous my name's Mike Jones from number 18... We'll see what happens eh.

Hung around to try and finish off a bit. Was dark now.

Two women passed and were dumb founded, a) at how much I'd done on my own and b) that I wasn't even a resident. Both thanked me which was kind.

Couldn't resist a "You're welcome" to some lads who used my clearing without a word, in fairness they then said thanks...

The Diary And Path Of The Warless Warrior

Partway through. By clearing I revealed loads of grit underneath.

Thursday 23/12/10

Up at 6:00. Damn body clock. Went out at 08:00 to clear the drive and pavement outside the house in exchange for grit. You're not supposed to use council grit on private driveways, but felt it fair considering the work I'd done. Did it predominantly for Emma's Nan who lives next door, but Emma's Mum had taken a fall the previous evening.

20 minutes in an Argos van went down and de ja vu kicked in. Eventually got them out too and tried my luck as I did with Fed-Ex.

Finished off what I wanted to do and came inside for a coffee. Just sat down when the sound of spinning tyres came from across the road. Hat, coat, gloves, shovel, coffee and out I went. Goodwill toward men and all that.

Walked down with Dianne to town to pick up the truck. Turned out it wasn't the alternator, was a loose belt and missing charge relay. A relay that had lived in the glove box since we'd bought it, as the previous owner didn't know what it was. Worryingly the mechanic noticed I was low on oil, the level just touching the bottom of the dipstick. Worrying as two weeks ago when I last checked it was just below the max line.

Still, god bless Lady Karma. The bill came to £75 opposed to the expected £300 +.

A Christmas cheque of £90 from a relative had cleared and that covered it.

Returned the favour of a lift to Dianne, then went on to my parents. Dad was concerned about picking up an Uncle from Bristol, so he took me up on my offer of driving them in our truck. Seemed fitting as it was this Uncle who'd sent me that cheque. Arranged to go back tomorrow and do the run around 13:00. Went on from my parents to see my best buddy Luke. His folks were very amused by my new winter hairiness.

Bloody knackered and starting to feel the effects of this cold I've picked up.

The Diary And Path Of The Warless Warrior

The Diary And Path Of The Warless Warrior

The Diary And Path Of The Warless Warrior

The Diary And Path Of The Warless Warrior

The Diary And Path Of The Warless Warrior

Parents New Wood Burner.

Friday 24/12/10

The run to Bristol was no problem at all despite the snow. Went via the A46 rather than the motorway for geographical reasons. A 74 mile round trip. Dad put forty pounds in the tank which was most generous as I used barely a quarter of that in fuel. This put the tank back to the level when we left Carmarthen. Uncle Ken, who we'd collected, slipped me a twenty pound note which I slyly passed to Dad. He was having none of it however and discreetly returned it.
Feeling very ill today and was exhausted when I left at 18:30.

Mum insisted I take their last three Lemsips and borrow a mini bottle of brandy to have with it.
Bless 'em.

My Parents House. (Note icicles over top right window)

Close Up Of Super Big Deadly Lollipops.

Monday 27/12/10

It has now become a standing joke in this family that every Christmas when asked "What would you like?", my reply is invariably "Peace and quiet". It is now so predictable, and perhaps depressing, no-one asks any more.

Well this year I came pretty damn close to getting it. Granted, it came at the cost of a stinking cold, but a streaming nose and nasty cough definitely make it easy for people to leave you alone. I made the effort to be present for presents. Trouble is, we have three Christmas days. One with Emma's Mum and Dad, one with Emma's sister and husband (plus kids) who come up from Farnborough on Boxing Day, and yet another at my parents the day after.

One major difference of this Christian Solstice over all those previous, is there are actually things we want and need. At the minute its warm stuff, but anything functional is welcome. Preferably something that enables us to produce something for ourselves.

I might even go so far as to say I'd be happy to trade my peace and quiet for a good thermal base layer...

The Diary And Path Of The Warless Warrior

The Diary And Path Of The Warless Warrior

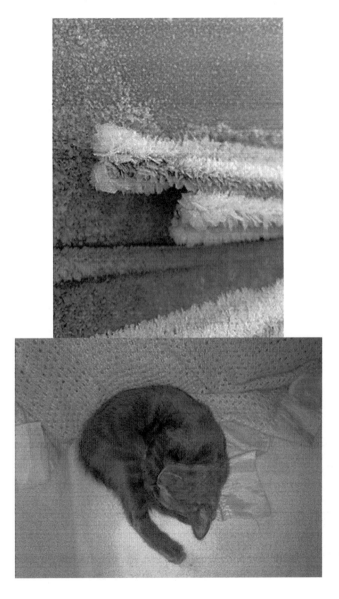

Tuesday 11/01/10

Returned to Lammas yesterday evening around 17:30.
Our stay with Emmas parents was prolonged due to a relay of
recurring illness. If I felt better, Emma felt worse and vice
versa. This happened daily, even now, although hopefully I'm
recovered and Emma is fighting off the remnants.

Before we left I asked Emma to check our car insurance, as I
knew it was up for renewal soon. Sooner than I thought. It had
expired a month earlier than I'd anticipated, 23/12/10 to be
exact. A fair few illegal and uninsured journeys had been made
since then.

This presented a real issue. Our premium had effectively
doubled from £460 per year to £880 odd. We couldn't afford
that, not even monthly.

The silver lining of this cloud might come in my solution. Why
not buy a days insurance? We rarely use the car as it is (in
comparison to most) and we could stand to save £500-£1000 a
year, more if you factor in fuel and wear and tear. The tricky
part could be when it comes to tax it, but aside from that, it
makes sense. Days we do buy insurance, we'll cram in as much
as humanly possible in shopping, treats etc. Seems win-win at
this moment in time.

Despite the hiccups, we're now settling back in. True to our
word, we did a massive shop before leaving Stroud and its
actually that which consumed most of our unpacking time.

Picked up my proof copy of *A Diary Of A Warless Warrior*.
Noticed a typo on the rear cover and first entry. My fault for
working on it when tired.

Since returning we've been greeted by rain. So much in fact,
the hardstanding the caravan is sited on is partially flooded, the

latrine trench is close to overflowing and the ground is saturated. The gloominess of the days hasn't helped motivation levels, nor the batteries. Have had little choice other than to remain inside and read. Extremely frustrating when there is so much I can be busying myself with outside.

The new cat stable...

Wednesday 19/01/11

Had a welcome change of pace Monday. Emma was booked in for an ultrasound scan at Haverfordwest hospital. With the car insured for the day, we did our best to make the most of it and be as productive as possible. The appointment wasn't until 14:30, so we had a couple of hours of mooching in the town centre. Bought a few bits in various charity shops, then headed to the hospital. We were in and out within an hour or so, everything having gone smoothly, and came away with a picture of our kidney bean.

The Diary And Path Of The Warless Warrior

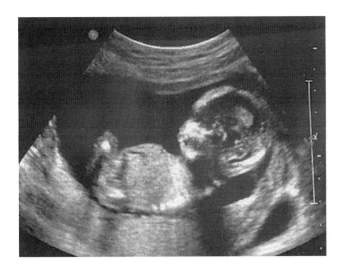

Next stop, top up shop at the supermarket. Kit arrived at the train station not long after and we gave him a ride home. Stopped in Clunderwen to pick up the last item - paraffin. With the return of Kit has come a break in the weather. Sunshine and clear skies, forecast to prevail until Saturday. It was an absolute pleasure to be back outside in glorious weather, marking out an orchard then constructing a woodshed. We didn't complete the shed as we ran out of light. And screws. Sourced some screws from Simon D, so our job today is to finish off and perhaps even extend the woodshed. The clear skies resulted in a bitterly cold night, but as always, this had given us a beautiful crisp morning thankfully with more warm sunshine.

The Diary And Path Of The Warless Warrior

Andy and Janes unveiled house.

Sunday 23/01/11

A cold nose and a full bladder tortures me until I rise, consistently around 06:00. The Sun himself is having a lie in and by the time he's dragging his lazy backside over the hills, I've already had a coffee, lit the woodburner, eaten a bowl of crunchy oats and cut a bucketful of kindling. To kill time and to keep warm on these crisp frosty mornings I take a walk along the plot perimeter. To make the walk as productive as possible, I bring along my air rifle. A vain hope. The land is devoid of prey. The only targets being two blackbirds. Two and twenty short of a pie so I don't bother. Plus I like them anyway for their appetite for aphids and other pests. As I make the return loop I spy three wild geese and a smattering of ducks. But they're on the millpond. Common, not private land. Being there is no one else around, there would be no witnesses to my

303

poaching. But they are on the water which is an issue. An issue for retrieval more than anything else. Still after three unsuccessful attempts thus far, I think they're safe.
Have added a scope to my wish list, with as large an aperture as I can afford to enable accurate shooting in low light. Then we'll see how safe those birds are...

Spent all of Saturday with Kit and mobile saw mill owner Adrian. Kit wanted his quota of timber milled 6"x6" and 5 meters long. By god they were heavy. The sort of weight that saps the strength in your arms to the degree that sheer willpower is all that prevents you from dropping the load on your toes. The next morning my arms were weak and sore. similar to that morning weakness that leaves you incapable of squeezing a grape.
Annoying, as we had the same amount again to collect that was left when we finished.
Going to bed at 20:00 used to be a rare occurrence...

The Hub Build.

The Diary And Path Of The Warless Warrior

The Diary And Path Of The Warless Warrior

Same job, helping a different plot holder.

Thursday 27/01/11

Progress on the woodshed has been sporadic to say the least. This is mostly down to welsh time keeping. Kit has a list of jobs to be done with heavy machinery. So far the contractor has never arrived when promised, even missing entire days. By his behaviour one could believe conventional working weeks do not exist and when working days do arrive, they never start at 09:00. In fact, working before midday is positively rare. I have a theory the Welsh are governed by the moon and decide working days/times by inspecting sheep entrails - just a theory. To fill in the hours/days of suspense we have carried bricks to the building site. Until we tire of it. Or build the woodshed. There is very little else we can do when you add in Welsh weather...

The Diary And Path Of The Warless Warrior

Not paying insurance or running the car has meant that for the first time in a very long time indeed, I have spare cash. Enough in fact to enable me to splash out on some choice novelties. So far I have splurged on a Hawke Sport HD 4 X 32 Mil Dot Scope. (watch out geese), a Stovepipe Thermometer., 2000 air rifle pellets, a Camo Padded Rifle Slip. and I have £40 with which to buy more. Am currently torn between Fireside Bellows. or going tactical and buying a Deben LEDRAY GL2 RED Tactical Air Rifle Light. or some warm slippers... Alternatively I can leave the surplus to accumulate.

Another caravan has arrived, adding to our row and fast becoming a terrace. The owner is another volunteer called Nick. A very likeable chap. I'd met him previously in November but completely forgot about his plans to return. Have helped him overcome the same obstacles we encountered upon our arrival. Namely decoding the solar panels and caravan electrics and cracking the enigma of installing a woodburner. Next on the list will be introducing him to gas bottle supplier and general Mr Build It/Fix It, Nick The Gas, but all in good time.

During our stay with Emma's parents over Christmas and New Year, I made a few observations that I have pondered over. Most of these are from drawing comparisons from our previous lifestyle and that of most. Often it is preached that households need to engage in certain practices to save money and be 'efficient'. There are so many buzzwords they almost lose all meaning. 'Carbon Footprint' 'Eco-This-n-That' 'Low energy ratings' etc etc. Then it hit me. The pieces slotted together and the answer was revealed. If a household were to follow these

'Green' practices to the full they would simply unplug as we have.

Water. Brushing teeth for example. I collect all our water by hand, and its heavy work consuming my body's energy. I don't like doing it too often. A cup 1/4 filled is all we need and use.

Gas. I physically have to get it. The bottles require manhandling and now cost over £50. Therefore filling the kettle with the amount of water you need saves gas and boils more quickly. The Pay As You Go system lets you keep tabs so no £300 surprises!

Electricity. No Sun, no lights. We use paraffin lamps and candles. I admit its not ideal in certain instances, but for the most part it suffices and costs little. By only switching on the inverter when we need electricity and by using low energy bulbs to extend the battery life, we have free electricity. That's with only a 60 watt array. To be uber efficient, we could reconfigure the electrics and run 12 volt LED bulbs.

Heating. Wood fuelled and therefore needs manual processing. When its cold we wear warm clothes and warm bed clothes. If you're like me, the two are nearly the same. I merely shed a couple of layers.

And there you have it. Disconnecting utilities and taking responsibility for your consumption and existence is the answer. Realistic? No way. Not in an urban environment. Possible, most definitely, and would be a most intriguing exercise.

Has been a feast for thought.

The Diary And Path Of The Warless Warrior

The Diary And Path Of The Warless Warrior

315

Tuesday 01/02/11

Meeting today. After reading Robert Harris' Lustrum, a
fictional account of the life of Cicero, I assumed my imaginary
toga and set out to join the senate.

I resolved to no longer sit in the shadows and watch, but to take
an active role and voice any concerns or opinions I may have,
with very interesting results.

At one point, after I had said my piece, the meeting had to be
halted and silence called to allow one of those present to shiver
and shake out her anger in the corner. This being to same
person who had visited us on Friday as Volunteer Co-Ordinator
to spread deceit and half truths. She even asked Emma why she
was here and what she contributed.

I feel no remorse at angering this woman as she angered mine.
Aside from this funny five minutes, all slid along smoothly and
Kit and I occupied ourselves laying bricks until the sun set.

Imbolc is nearly here and hopefully so is Spring. It can't come quick enough. There's the usual reasons, but my personal one is I have resolved to cut my hair much like a sheep is sheared. I have cultivated a wild mop of insulation with a notion of spinning it with wool to make something. That should gross people out.

Not shaving my face has been cheap, and I do kind of like my beard. But I feel it needs to go.

Diary intervals have slipped to around every three days which isn't acceptable for my memory nor my patience when writing. I put it down to getting slack in the slow winter with nothing to report or recount. Will be better I promise, yet again.

The slowly forming woodshed (1 of 4)

A lesson in brick laying

The Diary And Path Of The Warless Warrior

Dogsitting Teasel, whilst his master works on the Hub.

Wednesday 02/02/11

Insomnia struck last night. When I could take it no longer, I set out into the pitch black night, mist swirling in the light of the head torch. The spinning invisible drops of water caressing my cheeks as I walked to the barn.

Overloaded my brain with information. Read up on the Freeman movement, Common Law and the Magna Carta, joined justfortheloveofit.org (Mark Boyle's Freeconomist website), bought a share in Lammas and analysed the rules governing an Industrial and Provident Society. By 02:00 I had had enough.

We look after Nick's dog Teasel whilst he's volunteering, and this morning he brought along his copy of his 'Sovereign Declaration'. This is the first step to becoming a 'Freeman On The Land' as I understand it (and also completely different to the freeconomy movement!). All his learning has come from research on the internet, but also from a book titled Standing Under Freedom: A Foundation for Personal Empowerment. This book intrigues me greatly and I'm itching to exchange The Moneyless Man for it.

The late night really sapped my energy but thankfully the weather has been wet and windy. This not only signals winters demise, but just as importantly gives me a day off of sorts. Still moved large piles of wood and pushed a Volvo around but did less than usual.

Thursday 03/02/11

Each morning, I get up, empty my bladder and smoke a cigarette as I survey the sky and earth. On this occasion a cloudless night allowed Jack Frost a rather weak return. Next I clean out, reset, then light the wood burner, grab my rifle, and sit at the bottom of the field in hope that the Canada geese will take off within range. If the Mill Pond weren't off limits, or more accurately, if I and my family needed feeding, I'd shoot them on the pond if they ventured near the bank. Once again I was empty handed but not disappointed. Sitting alone, quietly on a beautiful morning is rewarding in itself.

Arranged with Nigel next door to execute four cockerels tomorrow, his wife wants it done simultaneously and we just have enough guns.

Planted 50 Italian Alder trees, had lunch, then completed the first course of bricks just before 17:00.

The clouds have rolled in on an unsettled and turbulent wind. To me this is an indicator of the seasonal change taking place. Nature shaking down and getting ready.

Not sure I'll hunt the geese tomorrow, not if chickens need murdering...

The first row of bricks completed.

Friday 04/02/11

A day of death. After more tree planting and moving piles of wood (during which time Teasel killed and ate two voles) we grabbed our guns and went next door to kill some chickens. No one was home but after a phone call to Nigel, one cockerel was marked for execution.

Taking his life was an experience I shall never forget. Cockerels are exceptionally tough birds and despite a well aimed shot through the side of the head, I wasn't satisfied. I reloaded and fired again. Blood poured from his wounds as he slowly reared his head, closed his eyes, and died. I know exactly when his life expired. He almost sighed his spirit away. This has enforced my resolve that should I hunt wild game and be presented with a shot, that shot has to be 100% satisfactory. The old cockerel has shown me how hard it is to deliver an instant and clean death. If that Cock did suffer, I hope he'll forgive me on the grounds his long happy life was far better than millions of his kind. His execution, under the Sun and Sky, on green grass, preferable to being slaughtered in a factory.

In butchering the carcass, I did my utmost to extract as much of the meat, and waste as little as possible, thereby paying the maximum respect to the life I had just ended. I definitely could not do what I did today every time I visited the supermarket. Imagine all the slaughtering and butchery you'd have to do when buying your endless meat based products. Burgers, sausages, nuggets, corned beef, gelatine, steak and kidney pies, etc etc.

Am extremely grateful for my profound experience today. Death has brought about a deeper respect for the miracle of life.

One of Emma's Bill Bailey Look A Like
Dolls...

Saturday 05/02/11

Ahh...Saturday. Generally, for me, no different to any other day. But this time Kit, the Boss, hitched a ride with Nick into Cardigan leaving me free to do as I wished. I wished for a wash. Frustratingly my quick fix on the bath plug let a large saucepan of freshly boiled water escape straight down the plug hole.

Stand up wash then.

Being that I washed in front of a mirror, and Imbolc has come and gone, I shaved off my Winter beard, instantly regaining my youth. Such a positive change in fact, I was kissed back into the bathroom by Emma. The kisses also put my ash toothpaste to the test. I was not impressed by the flavour, but its abrasive qualities left my teeth feeling the cleanest they've ever been. A couple of leaves of mint sorted the flavour problem.

With all my time off, I quickly got bored. So for the rest of the day I sawed and chopped up wood from the slab wood pile. These are off cuts and waste from milling and only three sawn up 5 metre lengths filled our cupboard and bathroom. Despite being wet with rain this wood is more seasoned than the other crap we bought and therefore burns better. Being larch it also burns hotter too.

Kit and Nick returned around 16:30, and we began cooking the 'cock' casserole.

Slow cooked in red wine with barley grains and vegetables, the meat was exquisite. Served with roast potatoes, it was a meal worthy of an upmarket restaurant.

Our bellies full of food, we passed the evening playing 'Farkel.'. Sometimes pronounced 'Fark - all' on low scoring throws! If like me, you have no idea what this is, broadly speaking, its a game of six dice. A player throws and different scores are tallied on the outcome. The throw has to include a one or a five. One = One hundred points and Five = Fifty. The other combinations of numbers and their values are similar to Poker. So you have Three and Four of a kind, a straight, Three pairs etc.

Since Imbolc on the 2nd February, the weather has been dreadful, with high winds and rain, but the cloud cover has kept the temperature comfortably high. Over 13C in the caravan and over 25C inside with the wood burner on. With that in mind, I am reverting back to sleeping starkas. Albeit with a hat on and a hot water bottle, just to be safe.

Will report back on whether its safe for the rest of the population to follow suit...

"We *did not* receive any messages sir, and Captain Blackadder certainly *did not eat* this delicious plump breasted ~~pigeon~~ cockerel"

Monday 07/02/11

For the past week we have been bombarded and buffeted by relentless high winds and intermittent rain. But just after midday today, as I was bricklaying, I photographed the moment the winds abated, the grey grumpy clouds moved on and the sun emerged.

The Diary And Path Of The Warless Warrior

I would like to think that the turbulent weather was part of natures process of ridding itself of the old season, and welcoming the new.

This afternoon, as I was demonstrating to a hapless piece of slabwood how easily my sharpened machete could hew large chunks out of it, I saw Kit and Cassie having what looked like a very serious discussion. She appeared to be in a 'fowl' mood, her husband had made a 'cock up' and we'd eaten the wrong bird. She wanted £10 in compensation, hardly a 'poultry' sum. Thankfully we hadn't executed an innocent bird. The delicious and full flavoured cockerel in question was indeed on Death Row, but meant for another table. Along with issues pertaining to the layering of a shared hedge bank, and accusations of responsibility for a new resident rat in their roof, I kept my beak out of it... Puns are fun.

Saturday 12/02/11

Have spent a fair few idle moments pondering the facts over and over in my head.

The wind was strong so I adjusted my position. Once fully satisfied I was safe, I proceeded to relieve myself against the earth bank. My LED head torch illuminated the droplets of rain that missed the back of my head. A strong lengthy gust forced me to lean back into the wind to regain my balance. At the same time the flurry of droplets increased, and started hitting my face. This was most strange being that the wind direction had remained unchanged. A dreadful thought occurred to me so I stopped mid flow. The 'rain' slackened off. I resumed the flow, the 'rain' increased.

The Diary And Path Of The Warless Warrior

Try as I might to dissuade myself from the truth, the only conclusion I can unavoidably draw, is that for the first time in my life, thanks to the gradient of the earth bank and the high winds, I do believe that I did piss in my own face.

In other less disturbing news my new purchase, a book called Basic Butchering of Livestock and Game. arrived and has been a fantastic resource. Accurately describing and illustrating not only how to dress a carcass, but best procedures to humanely despatch the animal. Also followed by some really intriguing recipes.
Aside from brewing some beer yesterday and gaining permission to hunt across the one thousand acre farm next door, this week has been mostly similar to the one before. Bricklaying predominantly. Nick planted some broad beans, erected his awning with my help (I identified the reason he was having difficulties attaching it to his caravan, was the fact he'd failed to read step 1 of the instructions), helped plant the orchard, then, possibly due to a late night last night, Kit reached his limit for the day. Early to bed tonight however, we're hoping to make the 08:00 low tide tomorrow and go foraging for razor clams.

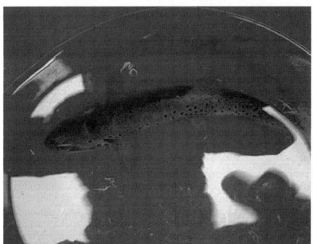

A fair sized trout fished from the leat.

Half expected him to start singing...

The Diary And Path Of The Warless Warrior

The Diary And Path Of The Warless Warrior

The Diary And Path Of The Warless Warrior

Tuesday 15/02/11

Up early Sunday morning to catch the low tide at Poppit Sands.

Foraging for Razor Clams - Pinch of salt, wait a few seconds, then grab the fleshy muscle as it pops up. All straight forward in theory, but got very complicated when we arrived...there weren't any.
Limpets and winkles it was. Oh, and a half dead baby octopus. Was fully dead when I placed him back in the water. His limp legs flailing and tangling in slow motion as the waves rocked his soft carcass along the ridged sand.
Stopped at an indoor car boot sale, was jammed full of the usual unloved detritus that clogs most peoples cupboard and loft space. Picked up an old set of Prinz 10x50 binoculars for

£6, plus a 3 prong candle stick holder for Emma. Was hoping to find some bellows and a hand grinder/mill. I swear I've seen one or the other at every previous boot sale, but not todays... Some top up shopping then back home to cook up a limpet and winkle stew. Limpets are rather rubbery when cooked and taste similar to kidney. Sadly, not a taste I like. Frances ate three but once she got one with a bit of grit/sand in it she gave up on the rest. Very please she tried them though.

Brewed up a Rice and Raisin wine I've named Cap'n Van Winkles Rice n Raisin Rum. Partly in honour of the day, but also to piss off Nick whose friends think his new beard makes him look like a fisherman.

The days catch.

Some sharks eggs aka Mermaids Purses.

The Legendary Cap'n Van Winkle Hisself...

Patience Kitty, It **will** ferment...

Monday - A long, hard productive day. Whilst dodging showers, some rain, some hail and some snow Kit and I managed to complete two sides of the building. Both the inside and the outside course. Working so low down really takes its toll on your back, but an hour of football and a shower soon cured that.

Today's meeting was very interesting indeed. Lots of emotion, background stories and underlying issues coming to the fore. I would invite all volunteers, visitors and shareholders to attend one of these meetings to really understand the challenges a settlement such as this faces.

I enjoyed being asked questions about my stay, how I view my role and presence. I especially enjoyed answering too! I often feel I talk at these meetings, but am rarely listened to, probably because I'm just a volunteer. Some are more guilty than others in the same way some are more 'equal' than others. A sad reflection on this so called Community comes with the next two scheduled days of consensus training. Despite being arranged months in advance and for the benefit of all residents, only four plots look set to attend. The others too busy with other things such as children's dentist appointments. Yet another sad day for Lammas and Tir-Y-Gafel.

Wednesday 16/02/11

Free reign for Nick and I today due to Kits absence. Began by planting up the hedge bank that divides Kits from Nigel and Cassies. Planted Hawthorn, Hazel, Crab Apple and Field Maple. This took us barely an hour and after planting more along the perimeter bank, we knocked up a privacy screen in front of the compost loo using two fence posts and the ground sheet of an old tent. Again, to shield the neighbours.

Nick left after lunch, leaving me bricklaying solo. Delayed due to both the weather and another volunteer enquiring about the availability of our old caravan. When he told us it was to enable him to stay with, and help Ayres, it was a done deal. Eventually I summoned up the strength and motivation to do two hours of back breaking brick laying. I couldn't have done it

better. Two rows in two hours using and only requiring all of just one mortar mix. Perfect!
Proud, but exhausted.

Sunday 20/02/11

Thursday was the second day of the consensus training. Took some time in the morning to cut and chop wood whilst the sun shone and the sky was blue. Sometime in the afternoon, after many coffees and relaxing, Emma and I planted some more hedging.

Friday I hung around outside helping Kit assemble another woodshed for most of the day. In the afternoon we mixed a small amount of mortar and built up the corners of the house. That way, all I have to do is join them up ensuring they meet the levels.

Saturday morning I hitched a ride with Nick into Crymych and bought £15 worth of water pipe and fittings. Between sorting and moving our little caravan for another volunteer, I rigged up the pipe. All connected, I opened the valve up and sauntered back to our static dreaming of running water and the luxury of a hot shower.

As I opened the door, my dreams evaporated. Emma was combating a cascade of water erupting from the boiler in the kitchen. Balls. As I'd feared over the winter and suspected after we took delivery of the van, the boiler had blown a pipe. Consulted Ayres on his recent repair job, and followed his advice of J-B WELD.

and Milliput. This meant a 24hr wait for it to cure.

Today I waited patiently for the repair to set. I busied myself with some track way maintenance for a neighbouring house, and Kit prepared to leave. After his departure, Nick and I murdered two more cockerels.

The first one was a beautiful dispatch. One shot to the back of the head and he was obviously dead. The other cockerel was none too happy and attacked Nick as he advanced to stick a knife in his dead chums brain.

The second was not so easy. Again, a shot to the back of the head followed by cartwheels, but he needed two more after that. Not good when Cassie and her son Davey were watching. Still, was all over very quickly and I think she was satisfied by my competence.

By now it was time to test my boiler repair - Boiler fixed, but now there's a leak and a crack in the pipe under the hot tap in the bathroom. Have got to wait another 24 hours whilst the silicone sets.

Will I ever get a shower?

The Diary And Path Of The Warless Warrior

The Diary And Path Of The Warless Warrior

Cap'n Van Winkles Walking Stick

Katy and Leanders Roundhouse, minus tarps!!

Tuesday 22/02/11

The boiler saga continues. Monday, I gave it a test. Tap sprang a leak again. Ok. Ditch the tap. Shoved in a stick to bung the pipe. Turned on the water, fired up the boiler. Lots of splurting and judders but hot water came through. Success? No.
My repair soon failed and once again the boiler began to leak. This time if silicone and milliput don't work I'll bypass the damn thing. My ideas are as follows;

A coil of black pipe on the roof will serve as the first stage primary heating, this I plan to then run to a section of copper piping behind the wood burner. In theory that should suffice and provide hot water all year, but as a back up I hoped I could run it to the gas boiler. This whole circuit will be closed I.e no header or expansion tank, protected by a safety valve.

352

One thought was to rc-use the cistern of the redundant WC toilet, but this would require an in-line 12 volt pump due to the pressure loss it would cause.

I have a vague idea how it will all come together and Simon D assures me that what I propose *could* work. I hope so. I want that shower.

Sunday 27/02/11

Have given up on the boiler. All looked promising until a drip developed and increased in frequency at an alarming rate. So far just having cold running water is luxury enough. My proposed alternative water heating project is on hold due to lack of funds. Costed the entire job and it came to £72 odd. That total was a combination of eBays cheapest and ScrewFixs. Hardcore bargain hunting. Still, £72 is £72 more than I can afford. I could buy the parts solely off eBay in dribs and drabs, but of course it would cost more overall.

I could save, however life finds a way of presenting other expenses of seemingly more importance.

The weather has been poor but forecasted to improve. Will be refreshing to return to the numerous outdoor projects requiring my attention.

The Hub, steadily progressing.

Life emerging all around us.

The Diary And Path Of The Warless Warrior

Garlic - The first of our seedlings poking
through.

Tuesday 08/03/11

The final shackle has been picked and I am free! After reading
Allen Carr's Easy Way to Stop Smoking., I'm the Non Smoker I
used to be. I could give you my opinion etc and tell every
nicotine addict its a must read before stopping. But it would
only benefit smokers who have realised its a mugs game and
truly want to break out of the cycle.
For a while I was a bit confused what to do with my tobacco. I
didn't want to keep it and hide it somewhere. If I gave it to

someone, that meant I could recall it as a debt. So I spread it on the grass. Ashes to ashes. Dirty filthy weed.

Despite only having stopped for 6 hours so far, I have noticed a marked difference in my breathing and performance. The iron bands I had once kept clamping on my chest are breaking away.

Yippee! I'm a Non-Smoker!

Not your average butchers shop...

The Diary And Path Of The Warless Warrior

Ying and Yang

Poisoning the orchard with the dreaded weed.

All gone.

Time to fight them English
landowners.

Thursday 10/03/11

Yippee! I'm still a non-smoker! The little nicotine monster is
doing his best but he is definitely starving to death. Allen Carr's
book is obviously a simple reverse brainwashing exercise
judging by the amount of repetition, but I will say that thus far
it has prepared me for all the hurdles and made this transition
or rather remission, very easy indeed.

My avian execution and butchery skills have obviously been
noted and recommended. My services have been requested on

another plot to despatch and prepare 3 non layers. With a deadline of Saturday evening, that means one in the morning, one in the afternoon, and one the next day. That's killing, plucking and preparing the damn things... hard work but at least we get one in payment.

Over the past few days I've been quietly getting on with planting rows of willow. As easy and therapeutic as this has been, I am glad to say it is nearly finished. Over half an acre planted in 2/3 days. Hope they do well and I haven't fluffed it. Am going to sleep well tonight.

Tuesday 15/03/10

Was asked to do some paid work work on Friday. Those 6.5 hours knocked 2 weeks off the wait for my £300 Webley Raider 10 Air Rifle. The wait now stands at 2.9 weeks. Handy, as its commonly said, the nicotine cravings pass after this time.

Thankfully the three non laying hens were despatched on a far more leisurely timetable than first thought. Using the method described in my Basic Butchering of Livestock and Game book proved to be efficient and effective, but a very different experience. Shooting provides physical and emotional distance, affording the marksman the luxury of not staring death in the face. Or holding it in his hands.
When using a knife to stick the birds brain, then opening the jugular, there is no escaping the effects of your actions, brought about by your desire. I literally held and extinguished life in my hands. It is not easy. In fact I would invite all those who

hunt with firearms to sample killing their usual quarry with a knife and their bare hands.

I for one never have, and certainly never will, kill for sport. It shall always and only be for the table. Mine. I still find it more unfathomable than ironic, that here I am in an intentional community, set up and run by people who wish to live off the land, and I am seemingly the only one prepared to hunt and kill my food.

Tomorrow Emma and Fran are heading to Stroud to visit family for a week, I wonder what it'll be like here home alone...

Its a dogs life...

...and a cats.

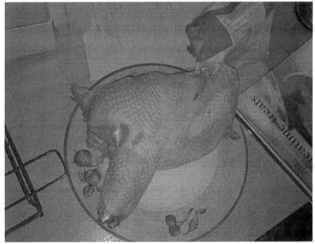

But not a chickens.

Saturday 19/03/11

06:06. Has been lonely without my family. As a consequence, I've done a fair few things. Took a bath, then reused the water to wash the dirty clothes I'd changed out of (particularly proud of that thinking), made briquette logs from cardboard using our press (they have since been drying on the wood burner), caught upon the blog, had a bash at some bread, then a soup... Ok, those last two were rather upsetting. Bread mk1 failed to rise. Possibly due to me misreading the recipe and adding two table not teaspoons of salt. Might help kill the geese... or could just dunk them in boiled eggs to save salting.

Boy! The eggs loved my second loaf. As soon as the two I'd boiled felt it, they shouted to their mates in the fridge. Overheard the ringleader 'hatching' a plan - when I next make a coffee, they're going to jump into the cafétiere in the hope they'll be boiled and I'll eat them with these sexy, silky smooth yet fluffy soldiers of mine. Eggbert Junior got so excited he rolled out of the fridge and tried to tell the chickens next door. So I boiled him up and smashed his head in...

Began soup around 18:00 last night and it was still cooking and 'softening' at 21:45. This failure could be attributed to the amount of ingredients.

3 x leeks,
1 x red pepper,
1/2 tin corned beef,
3 x carrots,
3 x potatoes,
1 x sweet potato,
2 x onions.

Quite alot for one man. Albeit by the time I surrendered and sadly slipped beneath the sheets, I was one hungry man...
Have had a deluge of new reading material lately, added to by the arrival of the library van, from which I borrowed 'Victorian Farm.', Matthew Reilly's 'Scarecrow.' and 'Good Old-Fashioned Teatime Treats.' (a hint to Emma that I'd like more puddings) Nick has lent me David Icke's 'Human Race Get Off Your Knees: The Lion Sleeps No More'.
Have only managed a quarter of 'Victorian Farm.' so will have to report back on the others.
An interesting, and I think, important observation in 'Victorian Farm.', is that the Victorians prolific resourcefulness and ingenious methods of recycling, stemmed from the simple fact that for the most part, they were very poor. As are many other cultures who are adept at wasting little. So there is the answer. The Big Wigs are listening. We have said we want more recycling in the UK and they're acting by making us poor. Cheers all you bankers as well as the equally guilty and greedy politicians. Nice one.

Rising from the warm, gassy depths.

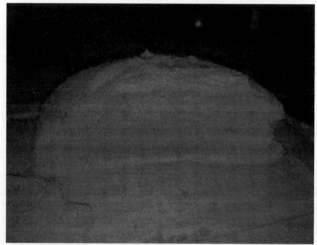

The accident.

The chosen one.

Monday 21/03/11

Estora - The return of the Goddess from the underworld, bringing new life with her.
Spring has definitely sprung but yesterday the weather turned wet and grey, dampening not only my pile of freshly cut logs, but my spirits also. Whilst a lot of what I do, I do on my own, I very much miss having Emma and Fran here to share it with. Only one more day of solitude left.

369

Lunch - MkIII Loaf

Whiled away a fair few hours continuing to dream about the many different air rifles I wish to buy immediately with all of my plentiful dream money. They are;

The Hatsan AT44-10:

Aside from the side lever cocking action, the 10 shot magazine and the fact its very competitively priced, I love the tactical thumbhole stock. Oh, and the brass magazine retaining bolt, and the gold plated trigger.

• Manual & Auto Safety. • Scope mount rail good for both 11mm and 22mm scope mounts. • 10-shot magazine (9-shot magazine in .25/6.35mm caliber) • Micro adjustable rear sight.

• Quattro Trigger: 2-stage full adjustable match trigger for trigger travel and trigger load. • Gold plated trigger blade

As wells as the detachable air bottle....

TRUGLO
Adjustable front sight

½" UNF threaded muzzle and fitted muzzle cap.

Detachable 180cc air cylinder for 200 bar fill pressure with built in pressure gauge. (230cc air cylinder in long version).

The Air Arms TX200 HC (Hunter Carbine).

Admittedly its Daddy is a rip off of the mighty Weihrauch HW77 of the 80's, and its a toss up between this and a HW97k,

but the Air Arms fixed barrel underlever rifle, wins on price.

The HW100FSB?

The HW100T?

The HW100K/KT/S/KS?

One of them anyway. Brand new these puppies are around
£600-£800. Justifiably so too. The best pre-charged pneumatic
rifle money can buy with a 14 shot magazine (x2) and silencer
included, its the dogs dangly bits. I would settle for second
hand therefore fate will decide which variant I get I imagine.

I am aware my list is PCP heavy with only one springer (two if
you count my rapidly ageing Hatsan MOD55S) I guess a
Weihrauch HW90 is an option, Employing the Theoben Gas
Ram system,

but then why not buy a Theoben? Too expensive? Well Hatsan do a gas ram version of the MOD 60s (my rifle but in .22 calibre) for approx £225, peanuts compared to a Weihrauch or Theoben, but probably for good reason.

If I had written this list earlier in the month, the dependable Air Arms S200 would definitely have been top,

but the Webley Raider 10 wins on price as well as possibly on pedigree.

Webley Raider 10.

Many would disagree in practice, but the theory is the S200 is a lightweight target rifle whereas the Raider is a solid hunter, hence my decision to buy a Raider. That's with scope, silencer (despite the already fully shrouded barrel) and gun slip for £310 inc p&p! (Lets hope the old adage "buy cheap, buy twice" does NOT ring true).

One cheeky little number I am also thinking about is the BSA Ultra Tactical Multishot,

although its single shot brother is £150 cheaper.
A fantastic weapon I have on loan at the moment in walnut stock flavour from Nigel next door.
Was out with it this evening, saw bugger all until in the fading light a duck flew very close on the other side of the hedge bank where I knew there to be a small pond. I spent forever sidling round to get a shot but it took off just in time. Being that the Ultra is pretty quiet and comes with a silencer as standard, a spot of goose poaching might become a damn sight easier.

The cats had the right idea. They refrained from a long ass walk and probably had more hunting opportunities than I did.

The Diary And Path Of The Warless Warrior

The Professionals. Greeted my return with
disdain.

Wednesday 23/03/11

04:00 Tuesday morning. Slipped out with the Ultra and blended
into the moon lit fog. Concealed by a cloak of mist, I finally
neutralised the superior eyesight advantage of the Canada
Goose. Taking my time, I approached the bank of the millpond
and knelt motionless. The frogs and toads were concealed all
around chirping merrily. The moon was exceptionally bright
(not surprising as I believe it might have been a 'super' moon)
and despite the clouded conditions, illuminated the scene with
an eerie white glow.

The Diary And Path Of The Warless Warrior

It was difficult to discern where exactly my targets were located, but my patience was rewarded when a 'loch ness' type neck loomed out of the mist. With the head in my sights, I followed the targets slow, lazy path and when I was satisfied of a clean shot, I fired. CRACK! Due to the water surface, the report from the muzzle was amplified massively. The head and neck disappeared from sight and my ears were relied upon to compute the situation. Slap, slap, slap, a slow, almost rowing motion could be heard. Then a honk. Had I mortally wounded but not killed the goose? Had I killed it with one shot, but was hearing the nervous death twitch and the grief of its mate? I think they were winding me up, and the honk was a prankster who couldn't hold in his chuckle. For when the sun rose later that morning and the mist had cleared, there were no dead geese, no wounded birds.

Still my nemesis eludes me...

Later in the day, very much later as it was gone 17:00 in fact. Emma and Frances returned from their week in Stroud. Whilst nice to see them, they have both brought coughs and colds and I am already feeling the first symptoms of having contracted it. Thanks Guys.

Today, in glorious sunshine, I laid another row of bricks whilst talking on the phone to my best buddy Luke who has just got back from Australia. Wants to live out there and I don't blame him. I would if I could afford the flights and were in his position. As it is, there are too many lethal critters for my liking for me to comfortably carry on living the way I am. I'm sure it could be done, but I'd rather go to a country where people still predominantly live off the land and Western culture hasn't yet killed off the traditional skills.

Have finally realised our cats full name; Eira Pookilicious Lovecrust. Eira Poocrust for short. Gunna get Fran to draw up her birth certificate on the morrow and make it official. Does the cat have a say in this? NO WAY! How many of us did?

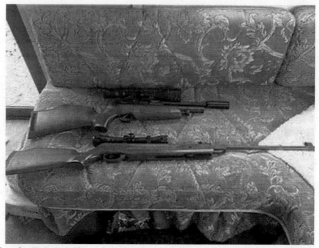

Nigels BSA Ultra Multishot .22 vs My Hatsan Mod55s
.177

My row on the outermost wall.

Friday 25/03/11

Helped out Jude yesterday. The idea was to construct a bender to use as duck housing. For me, a bender is no where near secure enough and when it turned out she had trees that needed planting (some bare root) there was no contest. This late in the year, them trees need planting! It didn't even matter where, as long as those roots were in the soil. when you live next to a tree surgeon-come-gardener, you learn about these things.
I have been very lethargic indeed. A combination of illness and the hot weather. Managed to watch Nick finish off a polybender, and partly aid spreading a canvas over his homemade geo-dome. In my experience and through researching these structures, the only ones that 'work' are those of the Bedouin style. Examples where people try to board them up and seal them seem to suffer many issues and problems.

The Diary And Path Of The Warless Warrior

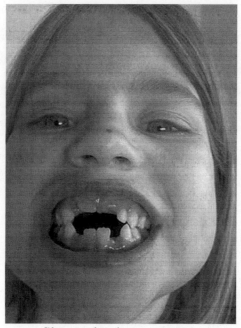

She used to be so pretty...

The Diary And Path Of The Warless Warrior

After a few dry days and two of hot sun, the ground is already cracking.

Wednesday 30/03/11

I have a knot in my stomach. Most likely down to nervous excitement, fear or the fact I took my eye off the ball and slipped back into smoking. (Albeit, at this moment secretly) Money worries have driven 60%-80% of this energy, the rest made up of the fear of not knowing yet desperately trying to formulate some sort of plan.

I am unsure if reading 'Standing Under Freedom' by TheAntiTerrorist is clarifying things for me or opening yet more doors and thereby overloading my poor little mind. That book is incredible but definitely only for a particular sort of reader. I *think* I'm ready to be enlightened....

The tax on our car runs out soon and the MOT not far behind. The windscreen alone will fail the car on its next MOT. This has forced forward our plans to return home for the baby's arrival.

Thankfully this hasn't posed a problem as we've been able to arrange accommodation.

The hub progressing daily.

The Diary And Path Of The Warless Warrior

A foraged salad of dandelion, sorrel and pennywort.

Home education...

I know you should let sleeping dogs lie, but what about cats?

Dorothy's hat squishing the Wicked WitchCat.

The buds of March

Saturday 02/04/11

The Day of Fools has passed and my awareness has increased with research. Have been learning about a variety of pieces of legislation and have dug up an exceptionally disturbing yet informative report on citizenship entitled Citizenship: Our Common Bond. This report, commissioned by Gordon Brown, documents the the transition from British Subject to British Citizen. I wasn't aware you could be a 'British Protected Person'! This status is seemingly a non-citizen who has been granted the protection and some rights afforded to a British Subject/Citizen. The report ominously calls for the revision of the Law of Treason to ensure all citizens know and abide by their responsibilities...

My research has also brought up some accounts of people who successfully retained the right not to register the birth of their child(ren). Very interesting indeed. Freedom is rather scary, especially to an institutionalised 'citizen' like me.

Oh! Watch out for the 'Citizen Corps'. A Hitler Youth sounding organisation proposed by the report!

The Terrible Two. Fran and Bea

Charlie's build next door

The Lammas owned woodland.

This exquisite resource and setting is so far under used and forgotten by most of the plotholders here.

Sunday 03/04/11

Mothering Sunday. A pleasant observation on Emma's part today, when she noticed that apart from the occasion Frances gave her a posy of flowers and cuttings, our daughter has been absent for near enough the entire day. Happily this is fine when one remembers that normally she spends the majority of her time in our company.

Through idle banter, Emma and I possibly stumbled on a disturbing truth. We are conditioned that we must 'Earn A Living', or is it earning the right to live? No other animal on Earth must do this and up until recently neither did humans. A musing I had today whilst sawing up firewood went along the lines of this. I was told in school that in the past "life was hard". Those who have attempted to replicate the

399

lives of those in various periods of history seem to concur. My question is two fold. One, without us individually sampling the methods of our ancestors, how can we truly understand what life was like? And two, does 'hard' necessarily mean 'less desirable'? Is comfortable and easy the right way for us to be heading? I understand seeking comfort. But the advice "live within your means" has never had more relevance in my opinion. It is advice I intend to follow and would invite others to analyse whether or not they are doing this.

Can you afford your fuel bills? The floor space you pay to heat and live on, the mode of transport you most commonly use, your methods of communication i.e mobile and internet tariffs etc.

When I've finished all this musing I give thanks that I have chosen to create a life where I can afford to spend my time doing so.

Monday 04/04/11

I cannot resist being amused by the contrast and transformation highlighted by the scenario I presently find myself.

I am seated at our table with my back to the kitchen. In front of me are books and beyond these sit Frances' friend Mirelle, Frances, and Emma. Apart from Emma, who appears to <u>never</u> cease knitting, we all have our heads buried in literature. The silence is punctuated only by Mirelles sniffing. She has a roll of toilet tissue in front of her, but seems content as she is.

The contrast and transformation of which I refer to can be explained thus;

'Normally when a van arrives near to where you dwell, the sky is blue and the Sun is shining. The vans arrival is hailed by loud unmistakable music. There is a rush, physical and emotional. Once you reach this van you might spend time deliberating your choice as you browse what is on offer, or you may already have a clear idea of what you desire.

Eventually, you return to your dwelling, the van departs, and one is hopefully left feeling very pleased with what has just occurred.

For most, this van is an Ice Cream van. For us, this van is a Library van. Make no mistake, as soon as it departs and I have consumed what it delivered, I too am left eagerly anticipating its return...

This time, rather than just stick to one flavour, I have gone for a few different tastes. 21st-Century Smallholder - Paul Waddington, The Medicine Tree - John Sharkey, Wales of the Unexpected - Richard Holland, and Men and the Fields - Adrian Bell.

Our little book club.

The Diary And Path Of The Warless Warrior

Continued my run of pearls of wisdom before going to sleep
last night. My mind wandered between the teachings of
Standing Under Freedom and the warnings of Nineteen Eighty-
Four. Inevitably the question arose in my mind "What, if
anything, can I do?""Is it too late?""What if it is too late?"...
It was then fates wicked sense of humour was revealed to me.
The ultimate irony that she does love so dearly...
So what if it is too late.
So what if we end up in an Orwellian society.
We can and most likely will use up all the oil on this planet. It
might be the cause or contributing factor in the decline and
eventual extinction of the Human species. Then what? And
here's the punchline...

In time, we will be turned into oil.

Friday 08/04/11

After a period of dark skies, fog, mist and much needed rain, the weather has returned to glorious sunshine and wonderfully warm days.
Spent yesterday and today helping out Jude with the repair of the door to her compost toilet. She and I have bartered and agreed to exchange time and skills in a mutually beneficial arrangement. Alongside many others, one thing I really like about Jude is her books. She has a great collection, nearly everyone of them interests me in some way. Currently the most interesting are The Complete Yurt Handbook by Paul King(would help with repairing the Yurt we've been given) and Make Your Garden Feed You by E.T Brown. They will have to wait however, as my current queue has lengthened with the arrival of Henry David Thoreau's Walden: Or, Life in the Woods..

From the little I have read of Walden, I can already see the author is not only ahead of his time, but also a man who shares my own thoughts and feelings on the subjects of our society, our past, our lives and our problems (which appear to stem from one or a combination of the aforementioned). I can tell that this is going to be a deeply thought provoking book.

I am still waiting to hear back from Kit after sending him and email of our thoughts a week ago. I deduce from this that things are perhaps hotting up his end with his first born due any day now. Without knowing his opinion of our thoughts and situation, I find myself often contemplating the myriad of potential outcomes, I will refrain from assaulting the reader with yet another of my lengthy and inconclusive lists.

Last night upon returning from a walk, Nick asked if I had read the note he'd left for us. Apparently our possible intentions have reached the ears of some of the locals who dropped by to view our static. It may transpire that our hand is forced somewhat if we are offered the £1400 it has cost us.

Above all else, today is the day I finally settled the bill on my new .22 Webley Raider 10 Pre Charged Pneumatic Air Rifle. I expect to receive it by the end of the week. Of course with most of the seasons now closed it should be just in time to be too late. Of course, that depends on how hungry I get...

The Diary And Path Of The Warless Warrior

The Diary And Path Of The Warless Warrior

The Diary And Path Of The Warless Warrior

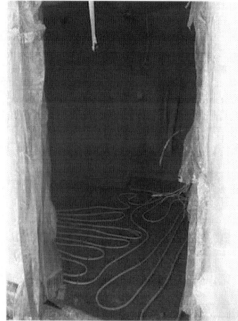

Under Floor Heating In The Hub

Has a very Mediterranean feel I think.

The Diary And Path Of The Warless Warrior

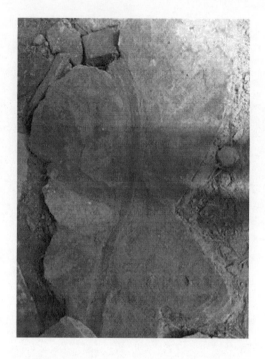

The Diary And Path Of The Warless Warrior

The Diary And Path Of The Warless Warrior

The Diary And Path Of The Warless Warrior

The Finished Article

The Hub

The Diary And Path Of The Warless Warrior

The Diary And Path Of The Warless Warrior

The Diary And Path Of The Warless Warrior

The purple sprouting broccoli seems to have survived.

A visit to Crymych and, for the first time ever, we managed to catch something happening at the market!

Saturday 09/04/11

Lobster coloured children maraud the site, some in varying degrees of zombification brought on by probable sun stroke. 25C at 19:10 should indicate the glorious weather we're enjoying. The hawthorn trees have burst with white blossom, nursed seeds and seedlings are now rocketing skyward. Some already falling prey to slugs.

Finally utilised a window of opportunity and moved the lattice, rafters and wheel of the Yurt under cover in the barn. A cursory inspection suggests with a little TLC and a new door if the original can't be located and we should have a half decent home. Presently that brings the count to three and makes logistic a further concern. We are definitely moving up in the world! Three homes owned outright after just a year. I am becoming quite the property mogul I fear.

Sunday 10/04/11

Henry David Thoreau's Walden. is rapidly becoming my bible and creed. If I were a believer in re-incarnation, I would swear that this man was myself in a previous existence. Although he was obviously more disciplined, not having impregnated a girl at the age of 17. I envy his freedom and fear the loneliness of the life he describes. Whilst I *could* abandon my now second time pregnant partner and young daughter as could any truly free being, I live in terror of my conscience. I am petrified of myself even if I follow what I know to be my life's true course and calling. My battle at this moment in time is to fight that calling with every fibre of my being until the day I can act upon it without regret. I know this to be pure folly. A foolish idea that will inevitably find me prostrate at the Devil's feet begging for another chance to live my life how I want to live it. I am aware I have always felt trapped and emotionally blackmailed into servitude of my 'lover' and it is my own moral code that binds my being and soul to her and my daughter. My daughter who has become a dear friend to me compounding my heartache further still. In the past, I once attempted suicide in the belief it would grant me the release I crave. I know now that the answer lies not in the darkness, but here in the light of this life, presently just out of reach.

Thoreau's work has become to me, akin to a pornographic magazine. Naughty. Taboo. Forbidden. I can only read a small portion at a time before my lust and envy grow too strong to bear. I flirt with the dream, then reason with my poor heart and convince my disturbed mind that what is portrayed within that books covers will never be mine.

It is in moments of bitter confusion like this that I pine for a cigarette. Could it be I enter a 'Self Destruct' mode? If that which I desire can never be mine then what point is there to this miserable existence?

If I were my own counsel I would advise myself to burn the book and never dare read another page. Ugly filth such as tobacco and nicotine are easy to live without, beautiful literature is not.

Tuesday 12/04/11

Embarked on a research mission yesterday. We purchased our days insurance at 10:10 and made a trip to the tip. Fran returned from a sleep over just as we got back. With our merry band complete, we went community shopping. That is, we viewed a place called Heartwood.

A really great community, very different set up to Lammas. They live almost as an extended family. Legally they are structured as a Housing Co-Op under the Industrial and Provident Societies Act.

It is a place we have been recommended, but they are presently at capacity.

In truth, an extended family is probably not what I am after right now, if anything, I'd rather downsize.

Whilst there, I mucked out a stable and helped build a cordwood wall. Emma helped Richards partner Staci mix cob that was used to plug the gaps. With that experience gained, today we built a cob oven!

The Diary And Path Of The Warless Warrior

The Diary And Path Of The Warless Warrior

The Shrew Hunter

The Diary And Path Of The Warless Warrior

The Diary And Path Of The Warless Warrior

The Diary And Path Of The Warless Warrior

The Diary And Path Of The Warless Warrior

The Diary And Path Of The Warless Warrior

Mixing The Cob

The Finished Product.

She Worked Really Hard.

The Diary And Path Of The Warless Warrior

Oh That's Right, No She Didn't... Lazy Beast.

Tah Dah! Some Call That Look 'Organic' Ya
Know...

The Diary And Path Of The Warless Warrior

A Tour By The Households Head Gardener.

The Diary And Path Of The Warless Warrior

Mixing Cob At Heartwood.

Didn't Take Long With Logs That Size!

The Diary And Path Of The Warless Warrior

A Very Tranquil Ty Bach...

15/04/11 Friday

Conversation and clarity. The morning of Thursday 13th April my legs took me where they wanted me to go. I spent time with Simon and Jasmine, Nick, the Hub volunteers and finally Ayres. Through these interactions I have been able to gain reassurance. Reassurance that we manifest our thoughts and realities. Understanding my position in this complex solar system of people, space, actions, words and atoms.

It was during this mornings wee that I was struck by the realisation I don't have a name. How can I hope to find something, namely myself, if it continues to remain unnamed? Why, that's like asking for directions when you can't recall where you're headed. It's not impossible but its a damn sight more difficult in my experience.

My legal and business name is on the front of this book. But that is merely the account name of the Government Issued Life Annuity. I need perhaps to research tribal naming traditions, and like Hercules, suffer the trials necessary in gaining my true name.

The Diary And Path Of The Warless Warrior

The Diary And Path Of The Warless Warrior

The Diary And Path Of The Warless Warrior

Frans New Hat

A Rather Delicious Dandelion Soup.

The Diary And Path Of The Warless Warrior

Mulching

The Diary And Path Of The Warless Warrior

The Diary And Path Of The Warless Warrior

Nicks Hand Plough, Good Fun And Labour
Saving.

The Diary And Path Of The Warless Warrior

A Budding Willow I Planted.

Saturday 16/04/11

Yesterday after jotting down a Diary entry, I continued in the
same vein as Thursday doing whatever I felt moved me. I again
visited Ayres, knowing he would be on his own and would
perhaps welcome the company. Interestingly he was having a
'silent' day. Happy to listen, just not to speak, the stickers
across his chest read. It seemed wrong to break the serenity, so
we sat, climbed trees and swang on ropes and a rope swing.
Finally, he gave me his iPod gesturing that I should listen to it.
On it was Eckhart Tolle's The Power of Now: A Guide to
Spiritual Enlightenment audio book. I closed my eyes and
absorbed the words. I understood how the 'now' or present

moment matters. How our outer purpose is whatever we happen to be doing and should be aligned with our inner purpose in order to bring true happiness and fulfilment.

It was with all these feelings in mind, that I demonstrated my desire to be treated, recognised and respected as the free and independent being I am and wish to be. I did this by having a cigarette. It caused Emma to exhibit ALOT of emotion and she disappeared for the afternoon. Did I feel guilty? No. I cannot own or be responsible for the feelings, thoughts, actions or deeds of any other being. I had realised, that in that moment, the only thing preventing me doing what moved me, was the thought and opinions of another.

I refuse to be ruled by any other than myself. Even if it is my partner. I explained my reasoning. At that time I also had no intention of returning to being a 'smoker'.

I believe that despite the upset, we have both benefited enormously.

To put it into context I shall quote Thoreau; "As if the sun should stop when he had kindled his fires upto the splendour of a moon or a star of the sixth magnitude, and go about like a Robin Goodfellow, peeping in at every cottage window, inspiring lunatics, and tainting meats, and making darkness visible, instead of steadily increasing his genial heat and beneficence till he is of such brightness that no mortal can look him in the face, and then, and in the mean while too, going about the world in his own orbit, doing it good, or rather, as a truer philosophy has discovered, the world going about him getting good".

To me this says, we are of the most benefit to others and

ourselves, when we do that which moves us and when we follow our true genius.

Rocket Stoving A Nettle Brew.

The Diary And Path Of The Warless Warrior

Cap'n' Van Winkle Banging Out Some Shanties.

The Diary And Path Of The Warless Warrior

Thursday 19/04/11

I have continued to endeavour to pay attention to, and do, that
which moves me. The hardest times are when I have bound
myself to another person and thereby to my honour. In
yesterdays case, helping another plotholder. Hard does not
mean unpleasant in this instance, indeed it never does mean
unpleasant. It stands to reason that when doing the bidding of
someone else, you are not free to do the bidding of yourself. I
was happy nonetheless. It was an arrangement of my choosing.
I was bolstered in this happiness when I stayed aware that I
was warm, fed, and dry. An important checklist!
If I ask myself why then couldn't I do this in the past in
employment and remained there contented? Well, thats easy, I
would've been kidding myself. "Truth is that which resonates
with the inner being" - Eckhart Tolle. I might have been warm,
fed and dry, but at the time I wanted more. My choices of
employment sometimes meant that whilst working I was none
of the above! I certainly did not want to be bound to a contract
that no longer felt of benefit to me. If a trade is perceived
unfair, we renegotiate and so, when my trade of labour cost
forty hours of my precious week and the compensation felt to
be inadequate, its time to renegotiate or cancel.

My air rifle has still not been delivered. After ringing to ask
when it would be, I was told by the driver it was not possible
until Wednesday evening. What bollocks. I've decided that
when he arrives I shall exercise my rights to the full.
Documenting any visible scrape to the product or packaging.
Actually testing the rifle in front of him before signing what he

wants, and by his laws <u>needs</u> me to sign. Needless to say, this will take time. I predict that he will not be released until at least 45 minutes have passed... Yes, I could admit that that would be thought to be vindictive on my part, but I know I don't want to accept a damaged or faulty rifle. Especially if it puts me at the mercy of a business man I do not trust. Far better therefore to take <u>my</u> time even if it costs him his.

I was very impressed by a victory for Emma and Frances yesterday. The local leisure centre have decided "No Card, No Entry". They wanted to take our daughters photo to put on an I.D card. Emma said "No" and with Jasmines help and backing forced the staff to concede it was wholly unnecessary and was nothing more than identity theft (Government condoned) and a breach of the right to privacy and confidentiality. That was definitely a victory, however small.

The Diary And Path Of The Warless Warrior

Toads Crossing At Night....

The Diary And Path Of The Warless Warrior

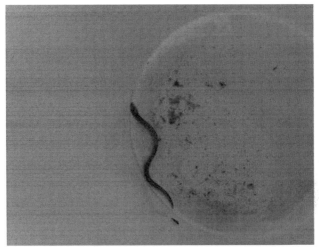

A Leech - An Inhabitant Of The Millpond

Cap'n Van Winkle Chilling Out

Wednesday 20/04/11

We are enjoying an extraordinary run of glorious weather.
Spent yesterday with Jude, Emma and a volunteer called Andy.
We tried to erect a yurt. This yurt demanded we listen to it and
would not yield to any command in the same fashion of an
unbroken horse. We started at 14:00. By 18:15 I was too tired
to carry on.
Nick jumped out on us from his caravan to pass on the news.
Kits son has been born by caesarean section and is healthy and
well. Well done Saara!

Throughout the colder months we talked of the need to get
some bikes and get out cycling. Only today did I realise I had
that opportunity thanks to a bicycle Kit said we could use. So I
went pedalling. Went pedalling nowhere particular with no
timetable and it was fantastic. I covered a fair distance in the

end and at different points experienced profound joy. Happiness so strong at times I laughed. I also saw things I couldn't have seen whilst driving. We travel too fast and thus it demands much concentration. I saw awe inspiring and beautiful details in the landscape, the hedgerows, the fields and even the roads themselves. I don't know why but there appears to be an awful lot of gloves littering these country lanes...

When my journey ended, my body felt no form of exertion. I could have been asleep for two hours. I was reminded of the energetic days of my childhood, when running or cycling meant nothing to my muscles. If anything I felt <u>energised</u> after exercise.

I am a child. A child who slept and dreamed a dream of what it could be like to be a boring adult.

This child is waking up.

This child vows to never be lulled to sleep like that again.

The Diary And Path Of The Warless Warrior

The Diary And Path Of The Warless Warrior

The Diary And Path Of The Warless Warrior

The Diary And Path Of The Warless Warrior

The Diary And Path Of The Warless Warrior

Purple Sprouting Broccoli Already Going To Flower.

What's The Time Mr Wolf?

Thursday 21/04/11

Exchanged labour with Ayres this morning. We loaded a trailer load of his wood from the quarry, and in exchange for using my truck, he helped load a trailer of my (Kits) wood and gave me some bio-diesel.
I was sorely disappointed my air rifle was not delivered as promised yesterday evening. So I did something about it.

I cycled the 13 miles to Cardigan to pick it up, prepared to cycle back with the rifle in an army canvas sausage bag. Trouble was, the rifle box was massive. I think the shop owner appreciated the trouble I'd gone to, so he drove me home! I left the bike and lock with him and I'll pick it up tomorrow on our day out. Needless to say I was very appreciative.

The ride there was daunting but by god it was incredible, much like the ride I'd done the day before only better.

It's all about the journey baby!

The Dream, Manifested!

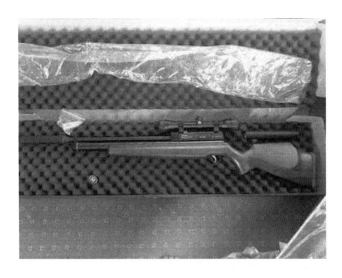

Friday 22/04/11

After doing "that which moved me" all week, I felt it was time my little family enjoyed a bit of movement too. To that end, we insured the Iron Horse and took a ride to Cardigan, Poppit Sands and then Cilgerran.
Emma had been given money by her mother and grandmother to treat Fran, so of course a walk to Yum Yums was in order.

As no one was going to treat me, I treated myself. To a fishing rod. (I'll admit to the white lie, Emma bought me some black Crocs).

After picking up the bicycle and buying a replacement indicator bulb (ours was on the 'blink') we let Fran loose on Poppit Sands.

By 14:00 however, the beach was filling up and I'd had enough.

Nearly every time we've returned from Cardigan I've seen a sign for Cilgerran Castle and each time thought it'd be worth a visit. So we did. I was wrong, it wasn't worth a visit. Not for £3.20 each or £9.20 for a family ticket. We saw nearly all of it by walking the public footpath along the perimeter. It was whilst doing this that I noticed another sign pointing to the 'Coracle Centre'. Again a bit disappointing as it was merely a block of toilets with information boards. That is not to say we were upset, definitely not, the weather was superb and the walk was most enjoyable.

The Diary And Path Of The Warless Warrior

The Diary And Path Of The Warless Warrior

The Diary And Path Of The Warless Warrior

The Diary And Path Of The Warless Warrior

The Diary And Path Of The Warless Warrior

The Diary And Path Of The Warless Warrior

The Diary And Path Of The Warless Warrior

The Diary And Path Of The Warless Warrior

The Diary And Path Of The Warless Warrior

The Diary And Path Of The Warless Warrior

Sunday 24/04/11

I really put the fishing rod to use, almost an entire day of fishing. I've come to view it almost in the same light as gambling. A promise and the excitement of a big payout or prize at the cost of something. In this case a day of my life. Fishing also failed to leave me too dejected despite coming home empty handed.

Easter Sunday. Resurrection. Life beginning anew and a fresh. I do have that feeling about the situation we find ourselves in.

We are leaving here in just over a months time. Until Kits return and we have a sit down chat, we don't really know anything beyond there. The birth of our second child could send any plans awry and be a catalyst for something else. Regardless of the uncertainty that perpetually lies ahead, I am at peace. The fearful future is of no consequence to me. I know that when Now comes, then will be the time to do. Do whatever needs doing.

I won't dwell on, but I would like to reflect upon our past 10 or so months here at Lammas. It has been our net after we leapt into the unknown. The inhabitants here have each held out hands to cushion the landing. Is that what they meant by 'Low Impact'? That thought makes me smile. Ayres and Marianne had a big role in our early time here for which I am eternally grateful. Kit and Saara have been equally generous and even in their absence I thank them both deeply for the lessons I have learnt whilst stewarding their land. Working with Kit has been greatly educational and enjoyable.

I am immensely excited about the position we're in and the immeasurable opportunities open to us. Where will we be if not here? I don't know GPS co-ordinates, but I do know it will be a place of our choosing. The reality, of our creation. A heaven to me could be hell for another, so in a family concessions and compromises need to be made.

I have faith. I have hope. And so should anyone.

The Diary And Path Of The Warless Warrior

The Diary And Path Of The Warless Warrior

The Diary And Path Of The Warless Warrior

Hot Cross Bun and Easter Nest Making.

The Diary And Path Of The Warless Warrior

Keiran Making His Mark.

A New Privacy Screen.

Cap'n Van Winkle After a Spot Of Chainsaw
Fishing.

The Diary And Path Of The Warless Warrior

The Diary And Path Of The Warless Warrior